Feeding Baby: A Cookbook

Simple Approaches to Raising a Healthy Baby & Creating a Lifetime of Nutritious Eating

CLANCY CASH HARRISON, MS, RD, LDN

Front Table Books
An Imprint of Cedar Fort, Inc.
Springville, UT

ISBN: 978-1-4621-1466-5

Published by Front Table Books, an imprint of Cedar Fort, Inc.
2373 W. 700 S., Springville, UT, 84663

Distributed by Cedar Fort, Inc., www.cedarfort.com

LIBRARY OF CONGRESS CATALOGING-IN-PUBLICATION DATA

Harrison, Clancy Cash, author.
Feeding baby / Clancy Cash Harrison MS, RD, LDN.
pages cm
Includes bibliographical references and index.
ISBN 978-1-4621-1466-5 (alk. paper)
1. Infants--Nutrition. 2. Baby foods. I. Title.
RJ216.H353 2014
641.5'6222--dc23
2014014712

Cover design by Erica Dixon
Page design by Bekah Claussen

Edited by Rachel J. Munk

Printed in the United States of America

10 9 8 7 6 5 4 3 2 1

To my children, Dylan and Cash, and their future children. May you always enjoy food and eat with your heart, mind, spirit, and body.

Contents

Foreword

When I was a little girl growing up in the era of the fifties and early sixties, fast food was not an everyday option. Hamburgers, sodas, and French fries were treats we only had access to on special occasions, when we went out to dinner or had a backyard barbecue, for which the ingredients were fresh and prepared at home. Most meals were not empty calories. Our meals were generally eaten together as a family with all of us seated around the table, where we would converse with each other and share stories from our day. Obesity was not an issue; Diabetes was not an epidemic. Today much has changed, and some of that change is to the detriment of our children.

I believe that *Feeding Baby* can empower parents to provide proper nourishment for their children, as well as the type of nurturing environment that children need to flourish. *Feeding Baby* is more than an infant nutrition book. It empowers parents to provide their children with not only food, but with love, patience, and trust. The author, Clancy Cash Harrison, a mother of two and a registered dietitian, helps lay the foundation for a lifetime of healthy eating habits by teaching infants and children to prefer and enjoy a variety of foods. Using the most up-to-date research, Clancy translates science into practical and easy-to-follow steps to raising a healthy eater—starting at birth.

Feeding Baby is in its own class of infant nutrition books—there is nothing else like it in today's market. Clancy encourages parents to teach their children taste by strategically pairing fresh foods with herbs and spices. She provides recipes, easy-to-read charts, tips, and solutions to increase flavor preferences by incorporating the use of all the infant's senses: taste, touch, sight, and smell.

Feeding Baby also helps parents focus on creating a positive feeding environment to maximize their child's nutrient intake. With a rise in childhood obesity, this book is a timely reference. Clancy helps parents understand the psychology of feeding infants and children, a child's ability to self-regulate calorie intake, and solutions to prevent picky eating and food jags. This book should be added to every parent's arsenal of parenting references.

In today's world, with kids and parents being bombarded with commercial messages from all directions, a guide for parents about how to prepare healthy foods for our young is both a service and a must! I admire the author's worthwhile goals and commitment, as well as the wonderfully imaginative and tasty offerings in her book. Her recipes make it fun for kids to eat delicious and healthy foods, and parents can enjoy the savory recipes too!

–Margaret Loesch
President & CEO, The Hub Television Networks, LLC.

Introduction

Feeding a baby can be overwhelming and intimidating. Trust me, I know! When I was a first-time mother, I experienced anxiety at the very thought of feeding my own child. I knew the choices I made would ultimately impact her health and lifelong eating habits. I knew that feeding an infant would require a lot more than nutrition. It requires patience, love, observation, trust, respect, creativity, and communication.

Feeding Baby is not just a baby food cookbook. It is a trusted resource that provides opportunities to teach flavor preference, create a positive feeding environment, and maximize nutrient absorption. This book will help you lay the foundation for a lifetime of healthy eating for your child. It does not matter if you decide to make homemade baby food, buy commercial food, or do a combination of both. This book will guide you in the process of raising a healthy eater, starting at birth. It will teach you how to reduce mealtime stress, and will give you peace of mind that your child is not just growing, but is also thriving.

In today's fast food world full of chemical additives, parents have more to worry about than ever while feeding their children. Not only do parents strive to serve "super foods," but they must also navigate the commercial food supply. *Feeding Baby* will show you how effortless it can be to serve wholesome foods that build dense bones, powerful brains, strong muscles, and a tough immune system. This book provides easy recipes for the entire family, while offering useful tips that can save you time and money.

With chronic diseases like obesity, hypertension, and diabetes adversely affecting children, it is essential to teach children how to appreciate healthy foods full of nutrients, color and flavor. Once you discover how easy it is to adapt this approach to feeding your unique infant and child, you will take comfort in knowing that your baby is receiving the best nutrition possible. This book is written for every parent and guardian who wants his or her children to establish healthy eating habits that will last a lifetime.

Chapter 1

Nutrition without the Numbers

As a mother and dietitian, I want exactly what you want for your children. I want them to be healthy. I want them to eat, but not eat too much. I want them to enjoy food without guilt. I want them to be adventurous in the kitchen. I want them to seek a variety of flavors and get excited about new foods. Simply put, I do not want them to be picky eaters, but healthy eaters.

I realize this wish list may seem unattainable to many parents. However, it is achievable. Yes, I said it. You can raise an adventurous eater capable of having a healthy and positive relationship with food. Many parents focus on nutrition alone. They focus on the numbers of nutrition—eating 5 fruits and vegetables each day, drinking X amount of breast milk or formula ounces per day, or eating the recommended daily calories. Parents should pay attention to nutrition. After all, it is vital for growth and development. The problem occurs when parents focus too much on the numbers. Nutrition is just one component of healthy eating. Parents should also concentrate on variety of foods and lifelong healthy eating behaviors.[1] We now know that a child exposed to a variety of foods has a better nutritional intake.[2] Instead of focusing on the numbers, parents can focus on flavor variety. This book will guide you how to incorporate the following while feeding your children:

- Teach "flavor preference" by exposing children to a variety of food, texture, and taste through a sensory-rich diet.
- Teach infants and children to recognize and appropriately respond to their feelings of hunger and fullness.
- Maximize nutrient absorption and intake by offering children a variety of nourishing foods.

Teaching Flavor Preference

Every parent, including myself, will spend countless hours teaching letters and numbers to their child. But how many of us actually teach our kids to taste food or to prefer food flavors? Teaching taste is just as important as ABCs and 123s because it sets the foundation for healthy eating habits. Flavor is not limited to the actual taste of food. According to science, flavor is made up of a variety of elements including taste, mouthfeel (the actual feeling of food in our mouth—texture and temperature), and aroma.[3] Flavor preference is taught by offering infants and children sensory-rich foods to eat and explore (you'll read more about this later) starting in infancy.

Most of us only think about our taste buds when we eat something with an intense flavor such as sweet, sour, bitter, or salty. We might also think about taste when we eat something we like or dislike. How often do you consider your baby's taste buds, or even your own? As parents we may overlook the sense of taste because we are so busy trying to be the best parents possible. We are occupied with teaching numbers, letters, words, animals, colors, and songs. Unfortunately, when we feed our children, we tend to concentrate on how much the child is eating, more than the elements that make up the world of flavor.

Parents are faced with many personal decisions without realizing the long-term impact they can have on a child's eating behavior. Tiny taste buds begin to form in the fetus, and further develop in infancy. The food choices we make while pregnant, breastfeeding, and during meals have the potential to expose an infant to a variety of foods. A pregnant or lactating mother's food choices mold a child's food preferences. Breast milk emits the aroma and flavors of the mother's diet. If a pregnant or breast feeding mother eats garlic, the child will taste garlic. If she eats curry, the child will taste curry. If she eats cumin, the child will taste cumin. Even more fascinating is that the infant will remember the taste of those flavors after birth, encouraging food acceptance in later months and years.[4–7]

One of the first choices you can make that will influence the infant's food preferences is the decision to breastfeed. The American Academy of Pediatrics (AAP), Institute of Medicine, and World Health Organization (WHO) all stress the benefits of exclusive breastfeeding for the first 6 months. Breastfed infants are more likely to accept new foods during the first introduction compared to a formula fed infant. This is understandable because a formula fed infant experiences one bland flavor day in and day out.[8–10]

Breastfeeding is instrumental to the introduction of a variety of tastes. The longer a child is breastfed, the more apt the child is to eat fruits and vegetables later in life. Therefore, lactating women are encouraged to eat a varied diet.[1–14]

As the child transitions to solid foods, the mother can continue to teach flavor preference by offering a variety of food. The more variety of food offered to the infant at 6 months of age, the better the acceptance of new foods.[15-17] The overall feeding experience of the fetus, infant, and child is heavily influenced by the dietary patterns and decisions of the caregivers.

Let's back up a minute and define the term variety. Most parents tend to associate variety with the idea of introducing different foods (asparagus, banana, apple, carrot). However, there is more to variety. If a child does not like carrots one day, don't give up. Just cut or prepare them differently the next time you serve carrots. In other words, carrots can be cut into long spears, coined, mashed, or diced. The idea of providing variety is not limited to serving new foods, but offering the same foods different ways. As the child becomes accustomed to the food he will be more apt to try it. Children will eat what is familiar to them. It is the parent's job to make the food familiar to the child through multiple introductions. However, it is important to ensure the texture of the food is age- and skill-appropriate (see Chapter 3).

A Sensory-Rich Diet

The basis of "flavor preference" is exposing the child to a variety of food by providing a sensory feeding experience. Sensory-rich food offers a variety of tastes, mouthfeel, and aroma while feeding in the appropriate balance. Food provides an opportunity for a child to use all of his senses (taste, touch, smell, sound, and sight). The acceptance or refusal of the meal is determined by those senses. Not only does the flavor of the food bring either disappointment or enjoyment, but the environment also determines the acceptance of the food. Depending on the child, a slight or drastic change in one aspect of the meal can change the entire experience. An uncomfortable seat, a very hot room, or an over-spiced dish can negatively impact the child's experience. It is important to consider all of the senses when creating a positive feeding experience.

Every adult knows the type of foods they like and do not like. Children are no different. They too have opinions about food, and also have stronger and more sensitive taste buds than adults, because unfortunately, adults lose taste buds as they age. Keep in mind—what an adult tastes is completely different than what a child tastes.

Parents should expose children to a variety of foods, but they should also respect their children's individual sensory preferences. Some children will be very sensitive to taste or texture (maybe even both). For example, my son had and still has a texture issue. He hated lumps in his yogurt. I learned to respect this preference and avoided lumps in creamy textures. He is now three and I continue to make slow changes in the texture of his food. Parents can determine an individual starting point for their child by simply listening to the child's verbal or nonverbal language. This might take time to see a pattern. If you can recognize a food aversion early and work slowly around it, you will be ahead of the game.

If you have a sensitive child, go slow. Mild, diluted, or smooth food may be more inviting to a sensitive child. Don't worry—all hope is not lost if your child dislikes a lump in their yogurt or cinnamon in their applesauce. It's just a starting point. Again, start slow and make very small changes. Select foods the child enjoys and add *very* small changes to the sensation. Avoid sensory surprises for the sensitive child—it would not be a good idea to give her plain scrambled eggs one day and a southwestern omelet the next. Just changing the amount of milk added to the eggs is enough sensory change to start with.

Remember that all children are different. They are different from adults, other children, and even themselves. Children change constantly. Their flavor preference will also change day to day. Just because a child liked a specific texture or flavor one day, does not mean she will like it the next. This is common behavior and should be accepted as normal, not picky (we will discuss this later).

from the mom tip

"Once my kids were cleared for solids around 6 months, I started introducing them to all types of foods. If it was something that was soft enough or I could cut small enough, they ate what we ate at the table. From an early age, my kids have had all types of foods: Chinese, Italian, Mexican, and more. I also made sure to introduce a wide variety of fruits and veggies. Now, years later, fruits and veggies still make up the bulk of our daily diet. Do they eat everything? No, because we all have our own individual tastes and preferences. But when my six-year-old tells people her favorite food is broccoli and my two-year-old begs for strawberries in the grocery store, that makes me pretty happy."

Megan Galko, Founder of
www.nepamom.com

Taste

Bitter, salty, sour, sweet, and umami (savory) are the 5 senses our taste buds recognize. Every nourishing bite will provide your baby with one taste or a combination of tastes which all influence each other. For example, something sweet can reduce the bitter taste of a vegetable. Knowing how to provide foods to maximize and balance flavor will encourage children to eat their vegetables. In other words, if you want your infant to benefit from the nutrients in a bitter food like leafy greens, you can add a sweet fruit like a banana to make the flavor more accepting. This is called "flavor pairing."

Let's face it—human babies naturally refuse bitter foods and welcome sweet and salty foods. It is not their fault—it is imbedded deep into their DNA. Our ancestors' survival was dependant upon their ability to distinguish between bitter and sweet foods. The most poisonous foods taste very bitter, making them unappealing. However, the sensation of bitter and sweet can vary considerably between each person due to age and genetics. Parents and children naturally have different taste senses and can influence the perceptions of picky eating as well. The good news is that flavor preference is learned, and strong flavors can be accepted over time.[18–20]

Not only do infants prefer sweet foods but they are also neophobic (fear of something new) about food. They have an inherent ability to protect themselves from potentially toxic foods. Don't worry—just because they fear new foods and love sweet foods, doesn't mean they can't learn to be healthy eaters. If your baby scowls at the taste of something new, don't give up after a couple introductions. Keep moving forward and concentrate on your willingness to reintroduce the same foods. Just change the flavor. Remember, changing the flavor is a simple as changing the texture (mash, finely dice, chop), adding an herb or spice, or serving it at a different temperature.

Myth Buster: Many pediatricians, grandmothers, and mothers recommend giving infants vegetables before fruit. It is thought that the sweet taste of fruit will interfere with the preference for bitter vegetables. There isn't any clear evidence supporting this theory. In fact, a variety of fruits and vegetables during pregnancy and breastfeeding lead to a greater acceptance of those foods by the infant. Also, repeated exposure to fruits and vegetables during weaning creates a preference.[16]

Mouthfeel

Texture, Shape, and Temperature

Our mouth has the ability to feel. It can distinguish textures and temperatures, which can have a dramatic impact on the flavor of our food. A food's texture has the ability to captivate and satisfy us at the same time. Creamy, fatty foods give us comfort, while crunchy foods give us pleasure at a social event. However, a food's texture can also repulse us. I know several adults who do not like texture combinations of creamy and lumpy. Keep this in mind when feeding your little one. They have opinions about texture, too.

Infants and children commonly refuse new foods because they may not like the texture or the taste of the food.[21] Parents tend to perceive this behavior as "picky."

There are a couple common mistakes parents can make when introducing a new food to their child. First, they introduce the same food the same way, each time. Second, if the child is still refusing a food after 2–3 exposures, the parent gives up and accepts a picky eater. I hope this book will empower you to take a different approach. If you refer to the chart on the following pages, 100 Ways to Serve 10 Fruits & Vegetables, you will see that there are many ways to introduce common fruits and vegetables, offering a variety of textures.

Temperature also affects the perception of a food's taste. It makes food more enjoyable, and can bring out the sweetness or even hide the bitterness of food. For example, letting ice cream sit out on the counter for a few minutes before serving will maximize its sweet taste. Even better—freezing bitter vegetables will take the bitter taste out of your smoothie when it is blended frozen and consumed immediately!

Infants should be introduced to a variety of temperatures, including cold, cool, warm, and tepid. Parents should avoid serving foods that are too hot—a baby's mouth is more sensitive than an adult's, and it is important to use caution. If a food feels slightly hot to you, err on the safe side and cool it more for your baby.

from the mom tip

"From the beginning of introducing solid foods at 6 months, we always gave Kaelyn the same things we were eating, by placing them on her tray and letting her decide whether or not she wanted to try them, without forcing or even encouraging her to do so. Many times she would either ignore the food, or just place it in her mouth for a second and spit it right out. I believe by doing this she learned that eating is a stress-free time where she can be just like mommy and daddy. Now, at 20 months, there isn't a food she won't at least try, and there are hardly any that she doesn't like."

-Jessica PhD, RD, Scranton, PA

100 Ways to Serve 10 Fruits & Vegetables

	Mashed	Finely Diced	Shredded	Chunky Chopped	Coined
Apple	warm applesauce	simmer in water with cinnamon	toss with pine-apple juice	cut and serve	cut and serve
Banana	with cinnamon or plain	cut and serve	freeze without peel, cut into thin strips when frozen	with dash of cinnamon	cut and serve
Broccoli	with cheddar cheese and cream	cook with pasture butter	shred stalk and slightly steam with pasture butter	steam with pasture butter	coin stalk and pan-fry in pasture butter until soft
Carrot	with dash of cumin or alone	cook	with cilantro and lime	cook with dash of cinnamon	cut and sauté with coconut oil
Pineapple	just mash	freeze and serve	cut very thinly and serve	dice with yogurt or cottage cheese	cut and serve
Squash, Butternut	just mash	cut and steam in orange juice	pan-fry with pasture butter or coconut oil	steam and serve	make large coins and oven roast
Sweet Peppers	oven roast, remove peels, and mash	cut and serve	sauté with olive oil	cut and serve	cut and serve
Peeled Sweet Potatoes	with cream	cut and steam in orange juice	sauté with pas-ture butter	steam with diced apples in apple juice	cut and pan-fry with pasture butter
Tomatoes	as tomato sauce over a favorite grain	with olive oil and balsamic vinegar	cut in half, remove seeds, cut into very thin strips	chill with basil and goat cheese	cut and serve
Zucchini	with cream and parmesan cheese	with basil and garlic	steam with pasture butter	stew with pasture butter	cut and serve raw with a dip

Chilled	Cooked	Strips	Dehydrated	Natural State (not necessarily to eat, but to explore)
chilled applesauce	oven roast with butter and cinnamon	cut and serve	serve apple rings	just an apple
chill and serve	use a yellow (not brown) banana, cut and brown in butter	cut into 2–4 long spears	serve banana chips	just a whole banana with peel
steam broccoli crowns, chill and serve	oven roast crown with coconut oil	cut stalk, steam, chill, and serve with a dip	cut stalk into thin coins	just a broccoli stalk with crown
slightly steam cut carrots, chill, and serve with a dip	cut and cook in broth	cut in strips, chill, and serve with a dip	cut into thin coins	just a carrot
cut into thick strips and freeze on popsicle stick	dice and cook in coconut oil	cut into very long sticks and serve	pineapple chips	just a pineapple
cut, steam, and chill	your choice	butternut squash fries (oven roasted)	butternut squash chips	just a butternut squash
dice and serve frozen	cut and sauté in pasture butter	cut and serve with a dip	pepper chips	just a pepper
steam, chill, and serve with yogurt dip	bake unpeeled	oven roast with pasture butter	sweet potato chips	just a sweet potato
cut and serve cold	slice and oven roast with olive oil and thyme	cut and serve	sun-dried tomatoes	just a tomato (large)
cut into strips, chill, and serve with a dip	slice into coins and oven roast with olive oil	cut, slightly steam	zucchini chips	just a zucchini

Aroma

The power of smell can be a surprising but wonderful sense at the same time. Imagine you just left home (after eating) and arrive at the shopping center around nine in the morning. Your objective is specific: a return or a purposeful coupon purchase. Unarmed, you inhale the sweet scent of cinnamon buns. They pull you in unwillingly. Suddenly, you are hooked and surprisingly hungry. This is called appetite. Technically, you are not physically hungry (stomach growls, dizziness, irritability, and so on), but that smell gave you a strong sense of comfort, memory, and pleasure. Unfortunately, companies know the power of smell very well and use it to their advantage. The good news is that you can do the same thing in the comfort of your own home.

A smell can also take you back in time to a special place. It will transport you to the minute—no, the second—you experienced that smell. A scented hand soap or candle might take you back to an exceptional childhood place. You might be in your thirties, but for a moment you are transformed into a young child on your grandmother's back porch—all because of a whiff of a sweet melon in an unexpected place. The sense of aroma is powerful.

The smell of food is thought to be responsible for a large majority of the flavor in food. I do know that a stuffy nose equates to very little taste in food (from personal experience). Using fresh foods and herbs in cooking could entice your little one to eat a variety of foods. If aroma potentially plays a large role in taste, memory, and appetite, we should not overlook it.

Adding fresh herbs while cooking can increase lifelong food experience and food acceptance. See the Baby Food Herb and Spice Guide on pages 16–19.

Food Fun

Sensory Play & Exploration with Food

As I introduce new vegetables and fruits to my children, I encourage exploration experiences. A child's decision to eat or try a new food depends on her sensory perception of the food. If a child does not like the way it smells, feels, or looks, she will probably not taste it until the food becomes more familiar to her.[22–25] To make food more familiar to them at the table and away from the table, I encourage my children explore the world of food on their own terms. I do this in various ways. I allow them to self-feed at the table or highchair, and I let them independently play with produce in its raw state. I read picture books to them with a variety of produce, and participate in structured play, which includes age appropriate cooking tasks.

For independent produce play, I simply put my child on a blanket and allow her play with her new vegetable toy in its natural raw state. I watch intently. Yes, I watch for potential choking, because children will put the produce in their mouth when curiosity gets the best of them—trust me. But I also watch because I find personal self-reward when they taste the vegetable. Not only did she discover the color, texture, and smell, but she also experienced taste because she wanted to try it. To increase familiarity with the vegetable, I always strategically feature the vegetable at the next meal.

Structured play is easy and fun. Instead of using paintbrushes for artwork, allow your child to use the ends of celery and other produce to stamp paint onto paper. For younger children, let them use their fingers to paint with the purées they eat at the highchair. As for cooking skills, I allowed my children to get active in the kitchen by 18 months of age. They would tear the kale leaves from the stems, peel cooked but chilled whole tomatoes, and peel their own clementines—or at least I encouraged them to try. Sometimes it was successful, and other times they created their own experience with the produce. Either way, we practiced familiarity away from mealtime.

I often tell my clients to think of introducing a new vegetable as meeting a new person. Imagine that your partner wants you to socialize with someone you dislike. Your partner pressures you to talk to her at the party, but you really do not like this person because she is bitter, pungent, and smelly. The more your partner pressures you, the more you distance yourself from the person.

Now imagine that your partner does not care if you socialize with this person. During your first encounter, you stand on opposite sides of the room, making no eye contact. At the second meeting, you walk past each other at the buffet table brushing elbows. During the third meeting, you exchange a simple hello. By the 11th meeting, you have grown on each other and actually enjoy each other's company.

The major difference between the two scenarios is your desire to meet this person on your terms. You were not forced to socialize. There is nothing more awkward than forced socialization, in my opinion. Using the second approach to introduce your infant or child to a new vegetable is easy, rewarding, and fun.

Simply put your child who can sit alone on a clean blanket with a favorite toy. Next to the toy, place a broccoli stalk. Step back and observe. You did it—you just gave your child the opportunity to meet broccoli on her own terms. Don't forget your camera, because you will want the picture of your child putting the broccoli in her mouth.

from the mom tip

"In the first months of starting solids, most babies are very open to new flavors. It is the best time to educate their palates by exposing them to as much dietary variety as possible. You can do it by including them in family meals to share the same food, with slight adjustments in salt content and texture, and by avoiding flavor-uniform baby food. At nine months old, my daughter enjoyed black rice with squid ink and seafood. At the "ripe" age of five, she still considers squid, octopus, and mussels her favorites!"

–Natalia Stasenko MS, RD, CDN,
Pediatric Registered Dietitian and
Founder of www.tribecanutrition.com

Remember, children explore their environments with their mouths, so supervision is necessary.

Note: While your children will explore and play with their food at the table—a normal and acceptable behavior until the age of two—you should separate intentional food exploration from meals.

Adding Flavor to Baby Food

Have you ever wondered what parents of other cultures feed their babies? From whale blubber in Alaska to spiced curries in India, infants around the world eat a variety of textures and flavors. Many countries follow their customs and traditions while feeding infants and children. Raising a child is a great time to get back to your culture. It is a time to teach your family history through flavor, and of course, love! Ask yourself: How can I get back to my culinary roots and further away from our commercially processed food world?

Food preferences develop early in life.[26] Don't be afraid to spice up your infant's life. I am not talking about adding a ton of spice or even hot seasonings. I am simply suggesting adding a little flavor to homemade or commercial food. A dash of cinnamon in oatmeal, a small heap of garlic puréed in meat, or a pinch of cumin in avocado can go a long way. Don't be afraid to open up your infant's senses, and have fun.

Make sure you read the allergy section of this book (pages 44–47) before introducing new foods, including herbs and spices.

from the mom tip

"Try not to let your food preferences limit what you will feed your baby. Let your baby explore all of the different flavors that God has created and break the cycle of picky eating."

Mindy, Cleveland, OH

To determine the best herbs and spices to pair with fruits and vegetables, refer to the Baby Food Herb and Spice Guide on page 16. This will help you add flavor to any food you serve your child. However, in this situation, more is not necessarily better. Start slowly and add small amounts of flavor to your child's food. Pay attention to your child's response, determine a starting point for flavor preference, and adapt the flavor gauge of your recipes. Remember, adult taste buds are weaker than infants'. Most of all, have fun and get creative!

10 Tips to Teach Taste

- Breastfeed exclusively for 6 months.
- Eat a variety of flavors while pregnant and breastfeeding.
- Add small amounts of flavor to baby food (commercial or homemade).
- Let your infant (who should be able to sit alone or with support) play with clean produce such as ginger root, celery root, carrots, beets, turnips, thick carrots, and garlic bulbs on a clean blanket. Please watch your child while playing with raw, hard vegetables because natural curiosity will entice them to put the produce in their mouth.
- Let your infant (6–24 months) explore her food at the table while feeding. Encourage self-feeding and exploration of foods without the pressure to eat them.
- Add variety within the same food.
- Throw out processed foods and replace them with natural whole foods.
- Replace sugar with fresh herbs in your entire family's food.
- Don't offer the same food two days in a row (unless you are breastfeeding).
- Get creative and explore new foods on your own. Look up new and exciting ways to prepare something that is on your staple menu rotation.

Baby Food Herb and Spice Guide

Herbs & Spices	Taste	Baby Food Pairing (food is in order of easy to more difficult to digest)
Basil Leaves	sweet, spicy aroma	apricots, peaches, peas, zucchini, carrots, blueberries, red bell peppers, broccoli, corn, potatoes, tomatoes, white beans
Caraway (dried seeds)	sweet, bitter	poultry, pork, apples, cabbage, onions, potatoes, sauerkraut, tomatoes
Cardamom (dried seeds)	sweet, bitter	apples, pears, sweet potatoes, yogurts, oranges, legumes
Cilantro Leaves	sweet, sour	avocado, yogurt, carrots, coconut milk, sweet potatoes, bell peppers, corn, cucumber, figs, potatoes, soups, stews
Cinnamon	sweet, bitter	poultry, bananas, apples, apricots, pears, yogurt, oatmeal, blueberries, pancakes, French toast
Chives	savory, spicy	avocados, egg yolks, fish, wild salmon, root vegetables, zucchini, potatoes
Coriander Seeds	sour	apples, egg yolks, beef, poultry, pork, onions, plums, potatoes, citrus, lentils
Clove (dried flower bud)	sweet	apples, pumpkin, sweet potato, squash, beets, red cabbage
Cumin (dried seeds)	bitter, sweet	apples, squash, beef, eggplants, lentils, chick-peas, beans, potatoes, sauerkraut, tomatoes
Dill (fresh and dried leaves)	sour, sweet	avocados, fish, carrots, zucchini, yogurt, cucumber, asparagus, potatoes, beets, cabbage, tomatoes, seeds: cabbage, onion, pumpkin
Garlic	bitter, sweet	poultry, lamb, meats, zucchini, tomatoes
Ginger	sour	apples, poultry, fish, passion fruit, pears, pineapple, mango

Herb and Spice Pairing	Tips
chives, cilantro, garlic, oregano, mint, parsley, rosemary, thyme	Avoid leaves that are drooping or blackened. Store for 2–3 days in damp paper towel or a plastic bag in the refrigerator vegetable crisper.
coriander, garlic, parsley, thyme	Caraway seeds can be bought ground but are best if bought whole. Grind as needed.
caraway, cinnamon, cloves, coriander, cumin, ginger	Seed pods will keep for a year or more in an airtight jar. Grind your seeds as needed.
basil, chives, dill, garlic, ginger, lemon grass, mint, parsley	Cilantro will keep for 3–5 days in the refrigerator vegetable crisper. Always use fresh and add to cooking at the last minute.
cloves, coriander, cumin, ginger, nutmeg, turmeric	Add early in cooking process.
basil, cilantro, fennel, parsley, tarragon	Chives can be chopped and frozen.
cinnamon, cloves, cumin, garlic, ginger, fennel, nutmeg	Buy whole seeds and grind as needed. Add near the end of cooking process.
cinnamon, coriander, curry, fennel, ginger, nutmeg	Clove flower buds will keep for a year in an airtight jar. Ground cloves should be dark brown. Add early in cooking process.
cardamom, cinnamon, cloves, coriander, curry leaves, fennel seeds, garlic, ginger, nutmeg, oregano, paprika, thyme, turmeric	Seeds will keep in an airtight jar for several months and ground cumin has a very short shelf life. Add early in cooking process.
basil, garlic, parsley cumin, garlic, ginger, turmeric	Store fresh dill in a plastic bag for 2–3 days.
most herbs and spices	Choose unblemished, firm heads without signs of mold or sprouting.
basil, cilantro, coconut, garlic, lime, lemon grass, mint, scallions, turmeric	Fresh ginger should be hard, plump, and heavy. They keep well in the vegetable crisper of the refrigerator for 7–10 days.

Herbs & Spices	Taste	Baby Food Pairing (food is in order of easy to more difficult to digest)
Lemongrass (lower part of stalk)	sour	poultry, fish, coconut milk, soups, stews
Mint (leaves)	sweet, tangy	carrots, peas, yogurt, asparagus, beans, cucumbers, eggplant, potatoes, tomatoes
Mustard (white seeds)	sweet	beef, fish, poultry, cabbage, curries, dals
Nutmeg (seeds)	sweet, bitter	egg yolks, poultry, fish, lamb, carrots, sweet potato, pumpkin, onion, potato, cabbage, spinach
Oregano/Marjoram (leaves)	bitter, savory	poultry, egg yolks, fish, lamb, meat, squash, zucchini, artichokes, beans, bell peppers, cabbage, cauliflower, corn, eggplant, potatoes, sweet peppers, tomatoes
Parsley (leaves and stems)	sweet, tangy	eggs, fish, most vegetables, lentils, tomatoes, lemon
Rosemary (needles, stems, flowers)	savory	poultry, fish, egg yolks, apricots, peas, pork, squash, beans, bell peppers, cabbage, eggplant, lentils, potatoes, soups, stews, tomatoes
Sage (leaves)	sweet, bitter, sour, savory	poultry, fatty meats, fish, goose, liver, asparagus, beans, cherries, pasta, potatoes, soups, stews, stuffing, tomatoes
Tarragon (leaves and sprigs)	sweet	egg yolks, poultry, fish, zucchini, artichokes, asparagus, potatoes, tomatoes
Thyme (leaves and seeds)	savory	meat, poultry, egg yolks, fish, root vegetables, beans, cabbage, carrots, corn, eggplant, onions, potatoes, soups, stews, tomatoes
Turmeric (fresh and dried rhizomes)	bitter, sour	meat, poultry, egg yolks, fish, root vegetables, spinach, eggplant, lentils, beans
Lavender (flowers)	sweet, sour, spicy aroma	meat, lamb, apples, peaches, plums, berries, cherries, oranges, potatoes, walnuts

Herb and Spice Pairing	Tips
basil, cilantro, cinnamon, cloves, coconut milk, garlic, ginger, turmeric	The stalk should be firm and not wrinkled or dry. Fresh lemon grass will keep for 2–3 weeks in the refrigerator if wrapped in plastic. Use in stir-fries. Add near the end of the cooking process.
basil, clove, cumin, dill, ginger, oregano, parsley, thyme	Bunches of fresh mint will keep for 2 days in a glass of water in the kitchen.
bay, coriander, cumin, dill, fennel, garlic, parsley, tarragon, turmeric	
cardamom, cinnamon, cloves, coriander, cumin, ginger, thyme	Nutmeg is best bought whole and ground as needed.
basil, cumin, garlic, parsley, rosemary, sage, thyme	Rub the leaves off the stem and store them in an airtight container.
basil, chives, garlic, mint, oregano, rosemary, tarragon	Fresh will keep in a plastic bag in the refrigerator for 4–5 days. Parsley can be frozen in ice cube trays with a little water. Don't buy dried parsley.
bay, chives, garlic, lavender, mint, oregano, parsley, sage, thyme	Fresh rosemary can be kept for a couple of days in the refrigerator. Add early in cooking process.
bay, caraway, ginger, paprika, parsley, thyme	Fresh sage leaves are best picked and used as soon as possible. Wrap them in a paper towel and keep in the vegetable crisper of the refrigerator for 2–3 days. Always use cooked and add at the end of cooking.
basil, chives, dill, parsley	Fresh tarragon can keep for 4–5 days in the vegetable crisper of the refrigerator.
basil, garlic, lavender, nutmeg, oregano, parsley, rosemary	Fresh leaves will keep for up to a week stored in a plastic bag in the refrigerator. Use at the beginning of the cooking process. Use dried or fresh.
cilantro, cloves, coconut milk, coriander, cumin, curry leaf, fennel, garlic, ginger, lemongrass	Store fresh turmeric in a cool, dry place or in the refrigerator vegetable crisper for up to 2 weeks; it also freezes well. Dried turmeric can last 2 years in an airtight container.
oregano, parsley, rosemary, thyme	Fresh flowers can be chopped and added to dough before baking. Infuse flowers in cream or milk. Chop flowers and fold into rice or use with meat. Fresh lavender will keep in a plastic bag in the refrigerator for up to a week. Dried lavender will keep for a year or more. Caraway seeds can be substituted for lavender.

Chapter 1 References

1. Ronette R. Briefel, Kathleen Reidy, Vatsala Karwe, Linda Jankowski, Kristy Hendricks, "Toddlers' Transition to Table Foods: Impact on Nutrient Intakes and Food Patterns," *Journal of The American Dietetic Association* 104, no. 1 (2004): s38–s44.

2. Carolyn J. Gerrish, Julie A. Mennella, "Flavor Variety Enhances Food Acceptance in Formula-Fed Infants," *The American Journal of Clinical Nutrition* 73 (2000): 1080–85.

3. Anthony Sclafani, "Symposium on 'Basic Mechanisms of Food Preference and Liking' How Food Preferences are Learned: Laboratory Animal Models," *Proceedings of the Nutrition Society* 54 (1995): 419–27.

4. Julie A. Mennella, Bernardo Turnbull, Paula J. Ziegler, Homero Martinez, "Infant Feeding Practices and Early Flavor Experiences in Mexican Infants: An Intra-Cultural Study," *Journal of the American Dietetic Association* 105, no. 6 (2005): 908–15.

5. Leann L. Birch and Jennifer O. Fisher "Development of Eating Behaviors Among Children and Adolescents" *Pediatrics Supplement* (1998): 539–49.

6. Leann L. Birch, "Development of Food Acceptance Patterns in the First Years of Life," *Proceedings of the Nutrition Society* 57 (1998): 617–24.

7. Julie A. Mennella, Coren P. Jagnow, Gary K. Beauchamp, "Prenatal and Postnatal Flavor Learning by Human Infants," *Pediatrics* 107, no. 6 (2001): 1–6.

8. Ronette R. Briefel, Kathleen Reid, Vatsala Karwe, Barbara Devaney, "Feeding Infants and Toddlers Study: Improvements Needed in Meeting Infant Feeding Recommendations," *Journal of The American Dietetic Association* 104, no. 1 (2004): s31–s37.

9. Arthur I. Eidelman, Richard J. Schanler, "Breastfeeding and the Use of Human Milk," *Pediatrics* 129 (2012): e827–e841, http://pediatrics.aappublications.org/content/129/3/e827.full.html.

10. Carolyn J. Gerrish, Julie A. Mennella "Flavor Variety Enhances Food Acceptance in Formula-Fed Infants" *The American Journal of Clinical Nutrition* 73 (2001): 1080–85.

11. Jane A. Scott, Tsz Ying Chih, Wendy H. Oddy, "Food Variety at 2 Years of Age is Related to Duration of Breastfeeding," *Nutrients* 4 (2012): 1464–74.

12. De Lauzon-Guillain, L. Jones, A, Oliveira, G. Moschonis, A. Betoko, C. Lopes, P. Moreira, Y. Manios, NG. Papadopoulos, P., Emmett and MA. Charles, "The Influence of Early Feeding Practices on Fruit and Vegetable Intake Among Preschool children in 4 European Birth Cohorts," *The American Journal of Clinical Nutrition* 98, no. 3 (2013): 804–12.

13. L. Cooke and A. Fildes, "The Impact of Flavour Exposure in Utero and During Milk Feeding on Food Acceptance at Weaning and Beyond," *Appetite* 57, no. 3 (2011): 808–11.

14. Catherine A. Forestell, Julie A. Mennella, "Early Determinants of Fruit and Vegetable Acceptance," *Pediatrics* 120, no. 6 (2007): 1247–54.

15. Gary K. Beauchamp and Julie A. Mennella, "Early Flavor Learning and Its Impact on Later Feeding Behavior," *Journal of Pediatric Gastroenterology & Nutrition* 48 (2009): s25–s30.

16. Leann L. Birch, "Development of Food Acceptance Patterns in the First Years of Life," *Proceedings of the Nutrition Society* 57 (1998): 617–24.

17. Julie A. Mennella, M. Yanina Pepino, Danielle R. Reed, "Genetic and Environmental Determinants of Bitter Perception and Sweet Preferences," *Pediatrics* 115, no. 2 (2005): e216–e222.

18. Anthony Sclafani, "Symposium on 'Basic Mechanisms of Food Preference and Liking' How Food Preferences are Learned: Laboratory Animal Models," *Proceedings of the Nutrition Society* 54 (1995): 419–27.

19. Catherine A. Forestell, Julie A. Mennella, "Early Determinants of Fruit and Vegetable Acceptance," *Pediatrics* 120, no. 6 (2007): 1247–54.

20. Maureen K. Spill, Leann L. Birch, Liane S. Roe, and Barbara J. Rolls, "Hiding Vegetables to Reduce Energy Density: An Effective Strategy to Increase Children's Vegetable Intake and Reduce Energy Intake," *The American Journal of Clinical Nutrition* 94 (2011): 735–41.

21. Suzanne Evans Morris and Marsha Dunn Klein, *Pre-Feeding Skills* 2nd Ed. (Austin: Pro-ed, 2000), 11.

22. P. Heath, C, Houston-Price and OB. Kennedy, "Increasing Food Familiarity without the Tears. A Role for Visual Exposure?" *Appetite* 57, no. 3 (2011): 832–38.

23. P., Dazeley, C. Houston-Price and C. Hill, "Should Healthy Eating Programmes Incorporate Interaction with Foods in Different Sensory Modalities? A Review of the Evidence," *British Journal of Nutrition* 108, no. 5 (2012): 769–77.

24. J.A. Mennella, S. Nicklaus, A.L. Jagolino and L.M. Yourshaw, "Variety is the Spice of Life: Strategies for Promoting Fruit and Vegetable Acceptance During Infancy," *Physiology and Behavior* 94, no. 1 (2008): 29–38.

25. Mary Kay Fox, Susan Pac, Barbara Devaney and Linda Jankowski, "Feeding Infants and Toddlers Study: What Foods are Infants and Toddlers Eating?" *Journal of the American Dietetic Association* 104, no. 1 (2004): s22–s30.

Chapter 2

The Power of Food

Food has power. Now let me rephrase: Food only has power that you allow to it have. The everyday decisions parents make in the feeding environment impact the balance of power between food, the parents, and the child. This chapter will provide guidance to help you empower your child (starting at birth) to eat a balanced diet incorporating variety, moderation, and proportion, setting the stage for lifelong healthy eating habits. In other words, you will give your child the power to eat (or *not* eat), shifting the power from the food to the child.

Expect Normal Eating Behaviors

"We taste food just as much with our heart as we do with our mouth, if not more."

-Karen Dornenburg, *The Flavor Bible*

One of my fears as a mother and dietitian was raising the dreaded picky eater. You know what I am talking about—the constant struggles and battles over food, or having a child that only eats chicken nuggets and grilled cheese sandwiches. I feared becoming a short-order cook or, even worse, bribing my children to eat vegetables. I agonized over the possibility of my children lacking adventure with food. I was concerned that my children would be malnourished and prefer sweet foods with very little nutrients. I was stressed because I did not want to fail my children.

I made a promise to my first child at birth. Literally, on the first day of her life, I vowed to never fight over food. Yes, I agree—another unrealistic goal. I admit I did have my doubts, but had high hopes all the same. Of course, I did my research and reviewed the latest evidence-based nutrition, medicine, sociology, and psychology journals. Two children later, I have never fought over food. No, it has not been picture perfect. And yes, I did have my worries, but that is normal.

When feeding children, the entire eating process should be considered. Family mealtimes nourish not only our bodies, but also our minds, spirits, and hearts. In other words, how we feed our children is just as important as what we feed our children. The feeding environment includes physical, social, and emotional interaction, and responsiveness between family members.[1] Refusing food or picky eating may occur when the mealtime is stressful both emotionally and physically.

A purposeful meal is a time for the giving and receiving of love. It is a time to learn

appropriate table manners, respect for others, and sharing of food. The mealtime is an opportunity for communication and socialization between family members, providing a sense of culture and tradition. It is a time to link generations. A meal offers an opportunity to teach family history and share recipes. Too often, family conflict arises over eating specific foods. Power struggles, frustration, and food refusal replace communication, respect, and nourishment.

Did you know that there is not an official definition for picky eating? Picky eating is something each parent perceives differently. What one parent considers picky could be considered normal to another parent. Typically, picky eating is associated with normal childhood eating patterns and behaviors. Understanding normal feeding behavior can prevent power struggles between parents and children.

Must-Know Normal Eating Behaviors & Facts (2-8)

- All children change their opinions about the foods they like or dislike day-to-day.
- Babies are born with a preference for sweet and salty foods.
- Most infants and toddlers refuse new foods.
- Children can regulate their calorie needs based on current growth patterns and age. Some days they like to eat, and others they are not hungry.
- Pressuring a child to eat is associated with poor eating habits and an increase of body weight.
- Forcing a child to eat food might set them up for long-term food aversions.
- Restricting foods high in sugar and fat increases the child's preference for them, and encourages overeating them when they are available.
- Pressuring children to eat puts them at risk of becoming overweight and overeaters, as they learn to disregard their own internal eating cues.
- Using food to comfort a child can cause the child to mistake unhappiness with hunger.

Creating a Positive Feeding Relationship

During infancy, a child reaches several feeding milestones. Infants develop the motor skills needed to eat (chew, drink, swallow, and self-feed) and they develop a lifelong relationship with food. The relationship an infant develops with food is heavily influenced by the parent's feeding schedule, behavior, and routine. The eating environment should be non-judging—full of love and fostering nourishment. Did you ever wonder why your mother's and grandmother's food tasted so good to you—even if other people didn't like it?

The comfort of their recipes soothed your soul and nourished your body. You found safety and security in each bite.

The feeding experience is a cooperative process including both the infant and the parent. Not only does the feeding experience provide the nutrients needed to grow, but it sets the stage for healthy development. A resource I use often and recommend to my clients is Ellyn Satter's theory called the "Division of Responsibility." I found myself very confused as a first time parent, and her work empowered me to focus more on creating a positive food connection with my children. The theory is basic and simple. Parents and children have specific roles in the feeding experience, which include:[9]

from the mom tip

"Children are born with the ability to self regulate, but feeding practices and food quality can negatively affect self regulation. For example, children who are asked to eat more or less of food by caregivers may stop listening to feelings of hunger and fullness. Kids allowed to graze on food may learn to eat out of boredom. And children given too many processed foods may not get full the same way they would with whole foods rich in fiber and protein. Additionally, children need more fat than adults do, so a very low-fat diet may leave a child hungry. The best things parents can do is offer meals and snacks at regular intervals, allowing children to decide when done."

–Maryann Tomovich Jacobsen MS, RD, founder of http://www.raisehealthyeaters.com and author of Fearless Feeding

Parent's Roles

- Cook and serve appropriate foods based on the child's developmental skills.
- Allow the child to eat according to his or her hunger and fullness feelings.
- Provide age-appropriate serving sizes of food.
- Provide regularly scheduled snacks and meals.
- Prepare food in a safe manner.
- Provide emotional and physical support.

- Make mealtimes pleasant.
- Teach table manners.
- Be a positive role model.

Child's Roles

- Decide what to eat on the plate.
- Decide how much to eat from the plate.

Allowing the infant or child the opportunity to self-regulate their food intake might be scary for some parents. I know this anxiety very well. I was a skeptical parent. But I now know that allowing self-regulating behaviors is one of the reasons I have never fought over food with my children. It is understandable why parents become concerned when their child refuses to eat. After all, we want our children to blossom into healthy individuals. Ironically, the more we push food on our children, the less they eat. Children will eat when they are hungry and refuse food when they are not hungry. They have the ability to self-regulate their food intake and do it very well.

Although children always need to feel safe and secure, they persistently push to become more independent. "No" becomes a very important word both verbally and nonverbally. The ability to express "no" without the experience of a negative consequence is an important life lesson. Using the "Division of Responsibility" allows the parent and infant the opportunity to practice using "no" several times throughout the day in a structured environment with limits. The ability to refuse food with the parent's acceptance ensures the feeling of support without fear of negative repercussions.[10]

No Fuss, No Cry

Pressure-Free Feeding Environment

Responding to "no" appropriately can be hard for parents when we want our child to eat. As a child transitions to family foods, their need to be independent will be evident as the child assumes more control over self-feeding. Unfortunately, many parents respond to food refusal by pressuring a child to eat. Pressuring is the process of forcing a child to eat more or less food than he wants to eat. Pressuring can appear in many forms:

- Breastfeeding or bottle-feeding on parent's schedule.
- Counting formula ounces.
- Preventing a child from exploring food with their hands and fingers.

from the mom tip

"Keep it fun so that your kids will try new things like vegetables. Remember, it takes 12 times before a baby actually prefers a new food, so don't give up!"

—Veronika, Maine

- Inhibiting a child from self-feeding at breast, bottle, or table.
- Bribing, comforting, and rewarding a child with food.
- Praising or cheering a child to encourage food intake. (For example, "Great job. You finished your peas!")
- Pressuring a child to eat food when he or she does not like it or want it.
- Withholding food from overweight children.
- Negotiating food for good behavior.
- Bartering dessert for healthier food.
- Hiding vegetables in purées and foods.
- Nagging your child to eat.
- Giving your child a sly look when he or she does or does not eat something.

Ultimately, if a child feels pressured to eat something, he will become upset. The pressure he feels sets the stage for a power struggle between the parent and child. Children not only learn to dislike the food they are forced to eat, but they begin to prefer and crave the foods they cannot eat. Forcing food on an infant can also teach the child to overeat, disregarding his normal feelings of hunger and fullness. In order to raise healthy eaters and prevent childhood obesity, parents should provide a variety of foods full of flavor, continue to feed nutritious food (high in calcium and iron), and teach a child to recognize his hunger and fullness feelings.[11–13]

from the mom tip

"I used to have a 'no thank you bite' policy until my second child came along and I saw that it could backfire with some kids, causing stress and more resistance to new foods. So now I gently encourage my kids to try new foods but don't require it or turn it into a power struggle. As a recovering picky eater myself, I know that they'll eventually try it given enough chances and enough exposure. And when they do, it won't be in an atmosphere of pressure or emotion."

Sally Kuzemchak, MS, RD, blogger at www.RealMomNutrition.com and author of *Cooking Light Dinnertime Survival Guide*

Accepting "No" and Setting Limits with Food

At this point, you might be thinking I encourage a "free for all" environment—giving the child complete control. Remember, you are the parent. You are the person who purchases the food for your family. You determine what is healthy or unhealthy for your family (which, by the way, is different for everyone). You set the boundaries.

Setting boundaries at mealtime is critical. Boundaries are set when we follow a daily schedule for feedings (three meals and two to three snacks), offer a choice between two to three food items, let the child help select the dinner menu from a pre-arranged list. For example, before meal preparation ask your child if they would like broccoli, carrots, or corn. Use your words wisely and avoid open-ended questions. If you want to include your child in menu planning, you can say, "Would you like to have chicken or fish tonight?" rather than, "What would you like to eat for dinner?" By setting boundaries and allowing your child the freedom to make decisions, you will teach them that they are capable of making decisions.

Proactive Coaching

One night at dinner, I realized I was practicing a proactive approach to feeding. It is simple, really. The idea is to be positive about food and expect your child to try new food without pressure. Here are a few common statements I use to encourage a healthy relationship with food:

"Since I know you really enjoy broccoli, I asked Grandma Harrison to make it for dinner tonight. I bet you are excited."

"It's okay if you do not like broccoli tonight, sometimes we are just not in the mood for broccoli. We will have it tomorrow for lunch."

"If you are not going to eat the broccoli, can I have it? I would like more and I am still hungry."

"Guess what Uncle Matt is making for dinner? Grilled wild salmon and creamed spinach—your favorite!"

"It is up to you to try the creamed spinach. I tried it and I really like it."

"If you are done eating, it is ok. Great job listening to your body."

"You must have been hungry. Great job listening to your body."

"Can you help me decide what vegetable to cook for dinner? Are you in the mood for broccoli, asparagus, or carrots?"

"If you are not hungry that is okay, but it is also your time to eat."

"Do you want to look in the refrigerator and pick out the vegetables for our salad?"

"How does the fresh cilantro, basil, and mint salad taste that Pops and Ya Ya made? I find it so refreshing and yummy."

"Of course you can try the candy. It is nice of your cousins to share. Make sure you tell me which is your favorite!"

On the flip side, parents can be counterproductive. I know—I have been there, and it takes patience. Here are some popular comments I hear my clients, family, and friends say to or in front of their children that can be counterproductive:

from the mom tip

"I like to put a plate of veggies, fruit, and nuts on an easily accessible table at snack time. That way my children are eating healthy while learning to eat a variety of foods. You can also bake homemade muffins with fruit and vegetables."

—Betty Jo, North Carolina

- "If you do not like your lunch, what else do you want to eat?"

Becoming a short-order cook teaches children they are not expected to participate in the family meal. They learn they do not have to try new foods because mom will make them anything they want when they want.

- "My child won't eat broccoli."

Why would a child eat broccoli after he or she hears this comment? The parent just set the expectation for the child to refuse broccoli, and the child will listen.

- "If you do not eat your dinner, you cannot have dessert."

Making a child clean his plate to eat dessert just encourages overeating. He learns that he must be full to eat dessert. He also learns that dessert does not fit into the meal plan. If you serve dessert, it should be a part of the meal. Remember, dessert can come in the form of healthy foods like fruit and yogurt.

- "Clean your plate; there are starving people in the world."

If this is your view, either make less food or plan to use leftovers at the next meal. Children should be able to self-regulate. Allowing children to serve themselves from a family-style setting is a form of self-regulation. Pressuring children to clean their plate is only encouraging over-eating.

- "Great job!"

I hear this a lot after a child eats all of her food. Parents mean well, but when they use this method, children learn that they are good when they clean their plates or are full from eating. This encourages over-eating.

- "I will bring chicken nuggets for my child; she is picky and only eats kid-friendly foods."

This is another popular statement that I hear too many times. If a child hears a parent say this, he will live up to this expectation. He will be picky.

- "I hate (insert any food)."

If a child hears a parent talk poorly about something, she will take on the same viewpoint. If mom does not like eggplant, it must be bad, right?

10 Tips to Empower Your Child's Eating Behaviors

- Encourage self-feeding and allow your child to decide what to eat and how much to eat.
- Expect your child to be adventurous with food.
- Respond appropriately to your child's hunger and fullness signals.
- Always provide familiar food with a new food or a "disliked" food.[14]
- Do not control food intake by attaching contingencies or pressure tactics. ("Clean your plate and you can have ice cream.")
- Offer food choices within limits.
- Provide meals and snacks at regular, scheduled times.

- Prevent the rut of serving the same foods by implementing a meal rotation plan. (Never serve the same foods more than once within a couple days.)
- Do not restrict sweet foods.
- Focus on the long-term goal of developing healthy eating habits and self-control.

Role Modeling

Children learn what is expected of them by observing the people around them. If you want your children to be kind and compassionate, you need to be kind and compassionate. If you want your child to eat vegetables, you need to eat vegetables. Your child will imitate the food choices you make. If parents eat foods high in sugar and empty calories, the child will too. Children are a direct reflection of our best and worst selves. I don't know how many times I have seen my daughter act out and see myself in her (as much as I hate to admit it).[15–17]

As a clinical dietitian, I constantly see clients with children who refuse to eat specific foods. If a parent skips the broccoli or speaks negatively about broccoli (or any food), the child will notice it. If you would like to see an eating behavior changed in your child, most often, you need to change that eating behavior in yourself. A child can be the biggest motivator for behavior change in a parent. Start making changes now in your eating habits so you can have a positive impact on your child's eating habits. A family-based approach to healthy eating is key to the development of lifelong eating habits in your child.[18]

from the mom tip

"I am the mother of three children (ages 5, 3, and 1). As a toddler transitions to solid foods, it is important to give the child the same food as the family eats, but in smaller servings. This allows the child to watch others eat and enjoy the same meal. Encourage your child to try different foods, but do not force the issue. I have learned that when a child is truly hungry, he will eat, even if a couple days pass with eating a few bites at a time!"

-Maria, MA, CCC-SLP (Speech Therapist), Maiden, North Carolina

Chapter 2 References

1. L. Alan Sroufe, "Early Relationships and the Development of Children," *Infant Mental Health Journal*, 21 (2002): 67–74.

2. Betty Ruth Carruth, Paula J. Ziegler, Anne Gordon, and Susan I. Barr, "Prevalence of Picky Eaters among Infants and Toddlers and Their Caregivers' Decisions about Offering a New Food," *Journal of The American Dietetic Association* 104, no. 1 (2004): s57–s64.

3. Judith E. Brown, *Nutrition Through the Life Cycle*, 5th ed. (Stamford: Cengage Learning, 2014), 281.

4. Leann L. Birch and Jennifer o. Fisher, "Development of Eating Behaviors Among Children and Adolescents," *Pediatrics Supplement* (1998):539–48.

5. Myles S. Faith, Kelley S. Scanlon, Leann L. Birch, Lori A. Francis, and Bettylou Sherry, "Parent-Child Feeding Strategies and Their Relationship to Child Eating and Weight Status," *Obesity Research* 12, no. 11 (2004): 1711–22.

6. Leann L. Birch, Jennifer Orlet Fisher, and Kirsten Krahnstoever Davison, "Learning to Overeat: Maternal Use of Restrictive Feeding Practices Promotes Girls' Eating in the Absence of Hunger," *The American Journal of Clinical Nutrition* 78 (2003): 215–20.

7. Jennifer Orlet Fisher and Leann Lipps Birch, "Restricting Access to Palatable Foods Affects Children's Behavioral Response, Food Selection, and Intake," *The American Society for Clinical Nutrition* 69 (1999): 1264–72.

8. Jackie Blissett, Emma Haycraft, and Claire Farrow, "Inducing Preschool Children's Emotional Eating: Relations with Parental Feeding Practices," *The American Journal of Clinical Nutrition* 92 (2010): 359–65.

9. Ellyn Satter, "How To Get Your Kid to Eat...But Not Too Much" (Boulder: Bull Publishing Company, 1987): 14–15.

10. Charles W. Slaughet and Alika Hope Bryant.,"Hungry for Love: The Feeding Relationship in the Psychological Development of Young Children," *The Permanente Journal* 8, no. 1 (2004): 23–29.

11. Irene Chatoor, Robert Hirsch, Melody Persinger, "Facilitating Internal Regulation of Eating: A Treatment Model for Infantile Anorexia," *Infants Young Child* 9, no. 4 (1997): 12–22.

12. Myles S. Faith, Kelley S. Scanlon, Leann L. Birch, Lori A. Francis, and Betty Lou Sherry, "Parent-Child Feeding Strategies and Their Relationship to Child Eating and Weight Status," *Obesity Research* 12, no. 1 (2004): 1711–22.

13. Ronette R. Briefel, Kathleen Reidy, Vatsala Karwe, Linda Jankowski, and Kristy Hendricks, "Toddlers' Transition to Table Foods: Impact on Nutrient Intakes and Food Patterns," *Journal of The American Dietetic Association* 104, no. 1 (2004): s38–s44.

14. J.A. Mennella and J.C. Trabulsi, "Complementary Foods and Flavor Experiences: Setting the Foundation," *Annals of Nutrition and Metabolism* 60 (2012): s40–50.

15. Leann L. Birch and Jennifer O. Fisher, "Development of Eating Behaviors Among Children and Adolescents," *Pediatrics Supplement* (1998): 539–48.

16. Judith E. Brown, *Nutrition Through the Life Cycle*, 5th Ed. (Stamford: Cengage Learning, 2014), 281.

17. Judith Sharlin and Sari Edelstein, *Essentials of Life Cycle Nutrition* (Sudbury: Jones and Bartlett Publishers, 2011), 38.

18. Mary Kay Fox, Susan Pac, Barbara Devaney, and Linda Jankowski, "Feeding Infants and Toddlers Study: What Foods are Infants and Toddlers Eating?" *Journal of the American Dietetic Association*, 104, no. 1 (2004): s22–s30.

Chapter 3

First Meal Fun

Baby's Readiness for Food

In two years, an infant's food intake progresses from an all-liquid diet to a solid food diet, which has an impact on her lifelong eating habits.[1] The transition to solid foods will be easiest if you do not rush food acceptance and allow your infant to set the feeding pace. Some babies will be eager to try new foods and others will be very cautious and slow.

Give your child the opportunity to explore food through touch, smell, taste, and even play. She will eat when she is ready. Let your child be your guide. If your child is not showing interest, that is okay. Take comfort in your ability to continue to offer her food without pressuring her to eat. The weaning progression (moving from a liquid diet to a solid diet) of an infant should include a balance of nutrients with a variety of tastes and textures. The foods you offer should provide sensory experiences while encouraging the development of self-feeding skills. An infant's ability to physically chew and swallow foods should be evaluated before the introduction of solids and during the progression of foods. Two important physical signs indicate that an infant is ready for solid foods:

- The infant can sit up and support her head.
- The extrusion reflex is gone. The extrusion reflex only allows infants to swallow liquid foods. The reflex is gone when the infant's tongue can transfer food to the back of the mouth and swallow. Around 6 months of age, an infant learns the developmental skills to eat solid foods.[2]

Other physical and emotional signs that your infant is ready to begin solid foods:

- Expresses a desire to eat by leaning into the spoon and opening her mouth when hungry.
- Communicates that the meal has come to an end by leaning backwards or turning her head away from the food.[3]
- Can chew food in an up-and-down motion.
- Shows an interest in your meal.
- Reaches for food and effectively puts it into her mouth.

Knowing when to start solid foods is important. It is also important to know when your baby is done eating or is full. Allowing your child to self-regulate liquid or food intake, starting at the very first feeding after birth, is critical and should continue into adulthood. These are signs that your baby wants to end the feeding sessions:

- Turns her head away from the food source (breast, bottle, or spoon).
- Spits food out.

- Shows an interest in other things.
- Cries.
- Arches back.
- Throws food.

An infant is not physically and developmentally ready to eat solid foods before 4 months of age. In fact, there are 60 countries that recommend introducing solid foods after the infant's 6-month birthday, and extensive research has encouraged many organizations to update their recommendations to exclusive breastfeeding for 6 months. However, the AAP (The Academy of American Pediatrics) committee does report that the introduction of solid foods between 4–6 months does not cause harm as long as the child is developmentally ready.[4–5]

Beginning solids at 6 months of age offers an infant more time to develop physically and build a stronger immune system. A newborn can digest solid food, but not as efficiently as an older child or adult. All babies develop at different rates. But after 6 months, most babies are typically ready for solid foods. If solids are introduced too soon, the baby will have difficulty digesting the food, potentially creating unpleasant side effects—gas, bloating, colic, rashes, and diarrhea.[6–7]

Breast milk is a source of immunity for infants. Babies who are exclusively breastfed (no solid food or formula) for more than 4 months have fewer ear infections and respiratory illnesses than babies who had an early introduction to solids. The longer the infant is exclusively breastfed, the more immunity can be acquired from the mother's milk. Solid food intake reduces the consumption and production of breast milk while increasing the exposure to pathogens in foods.[8–9]

First Food Dilemma

Deciding what first food to feed your child can be confusing because of the many conflicting professional opinions available for parents. According to the National Institutes of Health and The Academy of Nutrition and Dietetics, the order of food introduction has little, if any advantages. In general, a first food should be easily digested, nutrient dense, and age appropriate.[10–11] Popular first foods I recommend include: free-range pastured animal products (juicy poultry, juicy beef, and egg yolk), iron-rich oat cereal (see pages 62–64), cooked butternut squash, puréed peas, ripe banana, cooked sweet potato, ripe avocado, and other fruit and vegetable purées.

At six months of age, an infant is growing fast and has an increased need for minerals, putting them at nutritional risk. Specifically, iron, zinc, vitamin D, and omega-3 fatty acids have been identified as nutrient risks in U.S. breastfed infants. Nutrient deficiencies can potentially cause cognitive and motor loss, anemia, rickets, poor growth, weak wound healing, and a decline in vision.[12–14] To combat iron deficiency, the most offending U.S. infant nutrient deficiency, pediatricians often recommend iron-fortified infant cereals as a first food. If you choose an infant cereal as a first food, I recommend oatmeal above rice due to the high arsenic level found in infant rice cereals.[15] Please see page 67 for more information on arsenic.

The fast growth rate of an infant requires the need for more iron per pound of body weight compared to adults. The American Academy of Pediatrics lists meat as an appropriate choice as a first food, but this is also considered unrealistic. It may be unrealistic because of the cost and cooking skills involved in the meal preparation of meat, when compared to infant cereals. However, meat is very rich in iron and zinc, which are also easily absorbed when consumed from a meat source. Infants who are given animal sources of proteins as a first food have higher blood levels of iron and zinc than infants feed an iron-fortified infant cereal. Infants who eat puréed meat mixed with vegetables also have a greater absorption rate of the iron found in the vegetables.[16–19]

I always encourage my clients to reflect on their family culture, customs, and traditions when determining foods to feed their infant. Ask yourself: What do I eat? What do I want my child to eat? How can I incorporate traditional meals with flavor and texture? Voila—you have your answer. The recipes in this book concentrate on infant super foods that build powerful brains, dense bones, strong muscles, and tough immunities by maximizing nutrient absorption. Use the chart below to match the skill levels and the texture of food that is appropriate for your child.[20–22]

from the mom tip

"Nutrition should be a key consideration when introducing first foods. A nutrient of the most importance is iron as needs jump from .27mg to 11mg at 6 months and is essential for optional brain development. Puréed meats and iron-fortified whole grain cereals make good first foods that are rich in iron."

–Maryann Tomovich Jacobsen MS, RD, founder of http://www.raisehealthyeaters.com, and author of *Fearless Feeding*

First Foods Based on Developmental Skills and Self-Regulation Signals

Physical Skills	Eating Skills	Hunger Signs	Fullness Signs	Food & Texture
Able to lift head while laying down	Suckling and swallowing Recognizes breast or bottle	Cries/fussy Opens mouth during feeding	Refuses nipple by spitting it out Stops suckling Falls asleep	All-liquid Breast milk Formula As the child gets older, the feedings will decrease but last longer
Sits with Support	Sucks and swallows Moves tongue side to side Recognizes food Mouths foods Drooling uncontrolled Interested in biting and new tastes Teeth eruption Moves soft food back and forth with tongue Opens mouth for spoon Expect baby to explore foods and get messy!	Cries/fussy Smiles	Stops suckling Spits nipple or food out Falls asleep	Breast milk or formula are still primary source of nutrition Feeding begins and ends with breast milk or formula. First foods: Egg yolks, puréed juicy meats, puréed fruits and vegetables Use breast milk or formula to thin purées.
Sitter	Rakes food into a fist Uses upper lip to clean food off spoon Can drink from an infant cup Use fingers to pick up objects Expect baby to explore foods and get messy!	Reaches for food or spoon Points to food Moves head toward food Moves food toward mouth	Turns head away from food or spoon Distracted by other objects Slows down pace of feeding Pushes food away Stores food in mouth Closes mouth	Feeding begins and ends with breast milk or formula. Breakfast, lunch, dinner, and snack patterns begin to emerge Offer thicker and lumpy purées or soft food Add more texture, tastes, and variety

Physical Skills	Eating Skills	Hunger Signs	Fullness Signs	Food & Texture
Crawler	Moves tongue side to side Begins to chew up and down Self-feeds with spoon Self-feeds finger foods Holds cup Expect baby to explore foods and get messy!	Reaches for food Points to food Shows excitement	Pushes food away Turns head Slows down pace of feeding Stores food in mouth	Breast milk Formula Offer diced, chunky table foods Finger foods Continue to add different textures, tastes, and varieties Breakfast, lunch, dinner, and snack pattern is established. Avoid choking hazard foods: whole grapes, whole nuts, cherry tomatoes, hot dogs, popcorn, sticky foods, hard raw vegetables
Walker	Chews and swallows skillfully Learns to use other utensils Drinks from an open cup Uses both lips to clear spoon Begin to teach the difference between exploring food and table manners	Expresses a desire to eat Communicates wanting a specific food (sounds, words, pointing) Can guide parent to food and point	Communicates "no" with words or body language Throws food Plays with food Uses phrases or sign language for "all done"	Breast milk Formula Whole milk (>1 year) Finely diced, shredded, or soft foods with chunky lumps Continue to add different textures, tastes, and varieties Avoid choking hazard foods: whole grapes, whole nuts, cherry tomatoes, hot dogs, popcorn, sticky foods, hard raw vegetables

Size Wise

The amount of food an infant can consume depends largely on the amount of food a stomach can hold (stomach capacity). As parents, we should remember that infants and children have significantly smaller stomach than adults and even older children. The first meal around six months of age should be roughly one to two tablespoons, with one to two meals each day. Keep in mind, breast milk or formula are still the primary source of nutrition for this age of infants.

Infants have frequent and fast growth rates. A child's appetite represents their changes in growth, making food consumption very inconsistent. A general guideline for a serving size is one tablespoon per year of age.[23] For example, a one-year-old serving size should be one tablespoon. Remember that this is just a serving size, not the entire meal. The child should be offered 2–3 servings at a time (one serving of veggies, one serving of meat, and one serving of fruit). As the child advances in age and solid food becomes the primary source of nutrition, the feeding frequency will increase to approximately 7 meals (including snacks) per day.[24]

Allowing the child to self-regulate food intake should take priority over a parent's need to control food consumption or count calories. Calorie counting occurs when a parent calculates the number of ounces of formula consumed at each meal. It strikes when a parent assesses the amount of food eaten by the child. Calorie counting sets the stage for a stressful eating environment and poor eating habits. The serving sizes listed above should be used only as a point of reference.

Introduction of the First Meal

Introducing solid foods to an infant is just that—an introduction. Do not expect your child to eat lots of solid food in the beginning. It is not until after the first birthday that other sources of food begin to significantly replace an all-liquid diet.[25] Establishing comfort and ease with eating solid foods is more important than concentrating on how much your baby eats. Patience is important when introducing food for the first time. Remember, the infant has been swallowing liquids his entire life. Semi-solid or solid food is a new experience that requires understanding. Try to imagine this experience for yourself. Yes, I know you cannot remember the first time you ate solid foods, but try to imagine the experience. Better yet, ask your spouse to spoon-feed you at his or her pace. Humor me—I am serious here—try it! It is a great learning experience and you will find that it is *not* fun.

As adults, we have been feeding ourselves for many years. Eating is second nature to us, and most of us do not think about the act of swallowing or chewing foods (even though we should, but that topic could fill another book). For an infant, eating food for the first time can be fun or scary, depending on the parent's approach. Go slow. A new food is, well, new. Not only is the food new, but so is the process. An infant will most likely spit the food out on the first try. Take no offense to this—it is not a sign of dislike. It is also not necessarily a sign of fullness (especially on the first bite). It is just a new experience.

Your child's first meal should be fun for everyone. If food is not forced, and if you are relaxed, the infant will look forward to this transition. Choose a time when your baby is not fussy or tired, and a time that is earlier in the day. Feeding new menu items earlier in the day will help you identify any foods that make your child gassy or give your child an allergic reaction. If you feed your infant a new food in the later part of the day, you could miss an allergic reaction and end up with a sleepless night.

Be flexible. Again, let your child guide you on feeding pace and pattern. Try to have a flexible feeding schedule and allow your child to eat based on the signs of hunger and fullness, rather than on fixed times and amounts of feedings. Eventually, you and your child will establish a feeding routine and schedule as the infant becomes older (>1 year).

As you move through the feeding transition to solid foods, more and more foods will be introduced. Remember that it can take many introductions of a new food before your child will even consider putting it to her lips![26] Infants and children like foods that are familiar to them. Always introduce a new or disliked food with a familiar food. Continue to offer the not-so-favorite foods, but consider different ways to prepare them, and provide variety. Children will accept foods more readily when they are exposed repeatedly in a supportive environment without pressure.[27]

from the mom tip

"My daughter has been trying a variety of fruits and vegetables and I recently made an avocado purée for her. Her facial expression was one of dislike. However, I decided to let her put her hands in the purée, which she loved. I found that giving her the freedom to explore her food encouraged her to eat more bites of the avocado."

–Meghan, North Carolina

Top Ten Tips For First Food Introductions

- Always give a first food in the earlier part of the day, not in the evening, so you can identify an allergy when the child is not sleeping.
- Offer the food when the child is hungry, but not hungry enough to encourage frustration and food refusal.
- Spitting out food is not necessarily a sign of refusal, but a sign that the infant is learning to swallow.

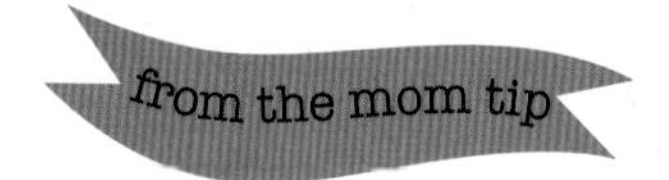

"I feel that my job is to provide [my daughter] with healthy options, but let her choose what she wants from the options I provide. So if she picks out the tomatoes—her favorite food—and doesn't eat the chicken, that is okay."

—Diana PhD, RD Springfield, OH

- Small portion sizes are best for an infant. Do not expect a baby's first meal to be more than a tablespoon.
- Expect a mess.
- Feeding is not a time for entertainment. In fact, you can increase the chance of choking while playing "airplane" and feeding the child at the same time.
- Go slow and follow the pace of feeding that the infant sets.
- Use skill-appropriate food choices. See pages 38–39.
- Keep it warm but not hot. The first food should be the temperature of breast milk, which is your body temperature.
- Stay calm. The more relaxed you are at mealtime, the smoother it will go.

Teaching Baby to Self-Feed

"They say fingers were made before forks, and hands before knives."
—Jonathan Swift

If you decide to feed your child his first foods between 4 and 6 months of age, self-feeding might not be an option. The purpose of spoon-feeding is to stimulate muscle development of the mouth and to help a child develop the skills to swallow. However, you can encourage self-regulation with a spoon by simply listening to your baby using these tips:

- Use a soft, shallow spoon to allow the infant to suck.
- Hold the spoon at eye level and let them see the spoon before attempting to feed them.
- Give the infant time to open his mouth and extend the tongue.

- Place the spoon at the tip of the tongue.
- Do not scrape food off of the baby's gums.
- Give the infant time to swallow.
- Only feed according to the baby's interest.
- If the baby reaches for the spoon, let her guide the spoon to her mouth.
- Allow the child to "teethe" on the spoon.

At six to seven months of age, most babies are developmentally ready to self-feed.[28] As parents, we know this is true. Just think of how many times parents scan the floor on the hunt to remove tiny objects (or, as parents call them, choking hazards). Infants love to put things in their mouths. The next time your child wants to explore, let her explore and discover food with her fingers.

Self-feeding is a wonderful way to experience food at the infant's pace. The process of self-feeding results in more food and nutrient consumption compared to an infant being fed by the parent.[29] Infants who practice self-feeding are also more likely to participate in the family mealtime, making meals more pleasant. An infant is developmentally ready to self-feed when she is able to demonstrate appropriate skills:

Anticipation: the infant expresses the need or want for more food by opening mouth, leaning forward, pointing, or reaching.

Eagerness: the infant is excited about food and mealtimes. The infant establishes the pace of the meal. The infant is involved both socially and physically.

Preferences: the infant has the ability to communicate likes and dislikes with verbal communication or body language (turning head away from food, and so on).

Reaching: the infant brings objects (food, toys) to mouth with hands.

Exploration: the infant enjoys exploring food.

Parents should be concerned with two goals during infant feeding: developing an infant's self-feeding skills and developing his positive relationship with food. If these two goals are met, the infant will develop an enjoyable association with mealtimes and food. Parents can empower their infant to develop hand-eye coordination, chewing

from the mom tip

"Naomi loves to explore and try new foods. When she was six years old I would cut cucumber into big slices and let her just gum it. She loved it. Since she was about 6 or 7 months old, I have been putting whatever we are eating (tofu, kale, rice, chicken, beans, avocado etc.) on her tray and just let her touch it, taste it, play with it. It is so fun to watch her explore."

—Diana PhD, RD Springfield, OH

skills, dexterity, and healthy-eating habits. Self-feeding offers the infant an opportunity to explore taste, texture, smell, and color while learning to self-regulate food intake (becoming a healthy eater).[30] The type of foods offered to the child can promote or inhibit self-feeding. Appropriate self-feeding foods include the following:

Dissolvable foods: These are foods that easily melt in the mouth.

Squashy foods: Very ripe or soft fruits, cooked vegetables, juicy poultry, and meat.

Safe foods: Avoid round hard foods and sticky foods (whole grapes, whole cherry tomatoes, peanuts, popcorn, hard candy, peanut butter).

Self-feeding is messy and takes time. Expect it and plan for it. Infants finger-paint with their food; they will smear food all over their face and in their hair. They will pour their bowl into their lap and even over their head. This is normal behavior. It is important to allow the infant to explore food and let go of the need to be neat. I put a sheet under the high chair to help with faster clean up.

Four-Day Wait Rule

Unfortunately, food can potentially cause an allergic reaction. It is important to incorporate a four-day waiting rule. If you have a family history of allergies, you may want to wait a week instead of four days. Either way, waiting at least four days before introducing a new food is important.

After every single new food introduction, examine the infant for allergy symptoms (see page 46 for a list of symptoms). The four-day waiting rule will help you identify the food causing an allergic reaction, allowing you to eliminate it from the diet. In the absence of symptoms, the quantity, frequency, and consistency of feedings can be increased and other foods can be introduced. Once each food introduction has passed your waiting rule, you can begin to mix foods into wonderful combinations.

The Poop Scoop

I never talked so much about poop until I had children. Poop seems to consume our days as parents. We count, inspect, and smell bowel movements—or at least I did, and still do. Yuck, I know. However, bowel movements are a great way to investigate the digestive health of the human body.

Newborn poop looks like black tar, and is called meconium. It usually passes within 24 hours of birth. As your baby begins to eat more food, the poop color and consistency will change. Breastfed baby stools are watery and look like a seedy mustard. A formula-fed baby's poop is greener, thicker, and more frequent than breastfed infants', but any shade of green, brown, tan, or yellow is okay.

An infant's bowel movements will change considerably once he begins to eat solid food. Most of the time, the poop will reflect the food just consumed. Not only will the consistency change, but you will also notice changes in color and smell. Color change typically reflects the types of fruits and vegetables eaten. Poop color will also change from feeding to feeding. You may even see undigested food. Some common colors of poop include: red (beets), orange (carrots), green (green vegetables), gray (blueberries) and tan (bananas). Typically, if I see undigested food in my infant's stool, I wait a couple weeks before I re-introduce the food—only to give me peace of mind that my baby is digesting that particular food fully.

Reasons to Contact Your Pediatrician:

- Very loose and watery stools with mucus and/or streaks of blood
- Chalky white stools
- Tarry black stools (after meconium has passed)
- Greasy or floating stools
- Constipation

Food Allergy and Intolerance

Currently up to 8% of all children under the age of three have a food allergy.[31] If you have a family history of food allergies, it is important use a wait rule when introducing new foods to your baby. There are several reasons to wait between new food introductions. First, an allergic reaction might not occur after the first introduction, but it may after a few re-introductions. Second, an allergic reaction can happen within minutes or even a couple days. Third, you do not want confuse any reactions with another food. Waiting four days between introducing each new food will help you successfully identify any potential allergens.

If your child has eaten new foods safely in the past, continue feeding those foods while you introduce a new food. After you introduce a new food, look for allergic reaction signs:

- Rashes
- Hives
- Itching
- Runny nose
- Wheezing
- Difficulty breathing
- Asthma
- Swelling of lips
- Abdominal pain
- Reflux
- Diarrhea
- Gas
- Vomiting

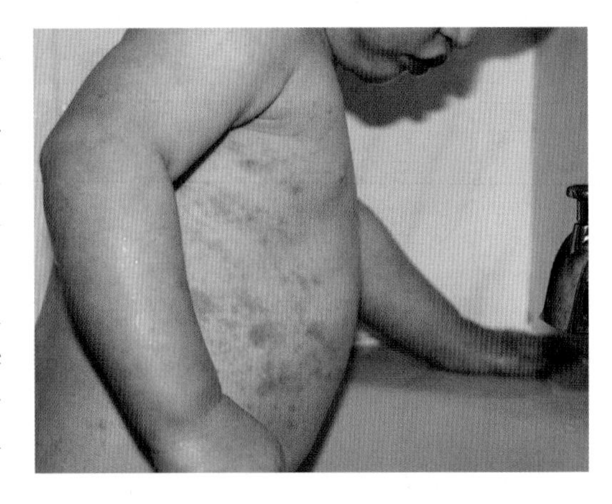

In the recent past, professionals recommended that parents hold off on the introduction of high-risk allergen foods. Now it is believed that the delay in the introduction of allergens might be associated with an increased risk of actually developing an allergy to those foods.[32] Here is why: The increased risk of food allergies and intolerances is associated with the amount and frequency of food consumed.

In other words, an older child eats more food more often. Scientists have also observed that children who have been introduced to peanuts by nine months of age had a lower prevalence of peanut allergies.[33] The most current guidelines to prevent food allergies according to U.S. Department of Health and Human Services are:[34]

- Diet restriction of high-allergen foods is not recommended during pregnancy.
- Breastfeed exclusively for 4–6 months.
- Do not use soy-based formulas to prevent allergies.
- High-risk infants (immediate family history) who are not exclusively breastfeed should use a hydrolyzed infant formula.
- High-allergen foods may be introduced at ages 4–6 months.

Food intolerance can be confused with food allergies, but they are different. Typically, food intolerances present the same symptoms as an allergy, but are not as severe or considered fatal (at least in the acute reaction form). Currently, the most talked-about food intolerance is gluten. Gluten is the protein found in some grains (wheat, rye, barley).

Gluten has gained a lot of attention over the past couple of years, because we are facing an epidemic of grain intolerances such as celiac disease and other diseases. Unfortunately, gluten is everywhere. Try walking into a grocery store or eating at a restaurant and avoiding gluten. It can be done, but you must become an investigator with a watchful eye because gluten is hidden in many foods. Not to mention that gluten does make our food fun and provides variety.

According to Sally Fallon, the founding president of the Weston A. Price Foundation, grains (all grains, including gluten) should not be given to an infant during the first year of life. After the first year of life, the introduction of grains should be slow. Grains should be prepared properly (fermented, soaked, or roasted) to maximize nutrient absorption.[35]

However, the current recommendations by the Scientific Advisory Committee on Nutrition (SACN), The Committee on Toxicity, and The American Academy of Pediatrics only address the introduction of gluten, which is:[36–37]

- Early introduction (< 4 months of age) may increase the risk of celiac disease and Type I Diabetes.
- The introduction of gluten should occur between 4-6 months of age while breastfeeding.

Believe it or not, in an era of childhood obesity there are alarming rates of nutrient deficiencies. Unfortunately, the majority of the nutrients consumed by children in the United States come from processed fortified food.[38–39] As a dietitian, it is appropriate to assume that many of my readers eat fortified grain products, making the recommendation to avoid grains a delicate subject matter. It is also important to consider the nutrient intake of the child. Eliminating high-allergen or intolerant foods without reactions or medical reasons may decrease the intake of vital nutrients. Removing foods from the diet in general also reinforces the behavior of rejecting food and limiting variety in the diet. My advice?

- Talk to your pediatrician.
- Introduce easily digestible foods at 6 months of age.
- Plan new food introductions 4 days apart.
- Assess for allergic reactions.

At this time, more long-term research is needed for food allergy and intolerances. Remember that every family and child is different. My first child had zero issues with grains, but my second broke out in eczema as soon as a piece of wheat hit his little lips. My second child did not eat wheat or gluten for the 18 months of his life. Going into his second year and part of his third year, he ate very limited amounts of wheat.

The bottom line is to be vigilant. I constantly and closely observed for allergic or intolerant reactions. I treated each child differently and consulted with my pediatrician. I recommend the same for you, but I also recommend a meeting with your local registered dietitian. There are many foods an infant can eat before the age of one without grains, if you choose this route. Refer to the Nourishing Foods Chart on page 57 to get the most out of your nutrition and minimize processed food intake. Don't forget to check out the recipes in this book for more wonderful ideas! Out of respect for all parental choices, I am including recipes for everyone to enjoy with tips to make them gluten-free (if possible).

Chapter 3 References

1. Barbara Devaney, Laura Kalb, Ronette Briefel, Teresa Zavitsky-Novak, Nancy Clusen, and Paula Ziegler, "Feeding Infants and Toddlers Study: Overview of the Study Design," *Journal of The American Dietetic Association* 104, no. 1 (2004): s8–s13.

2. Lewis P. Lipsitt, Charles Crook and Carolyn A. Booth, "The Transitional Infant: Behavioral Development and Feeding," *The American Journal of Clinical Nutrition*, 41 (1985): 485–96.

3. Samual Fomon, "Feeding Normal Infants: Rationale for Recommendations," *Journal of the American Dietetic Association* 101, (2001): 1002–5.

4. Judith Sharlin and Sari Edelstein, *Essentials of Life Cycle Nutrition* (Sudbury: Jones and Bartlett Publishers, 2011), 36.

5. Judith Sharlin and Sari Edelstein, *Essentials of Life Cycle Nutrition* (Sudbury: Jones and Bartlett Publishers, 2011), 37.

6. Balba Kurins Gillard, Janet A. Simbala, and Lee Goodglick, "Reference Intervals for Amylase Isoenzymes in Serum and Plasma of Infants and children," *Clinical Chemistry* 29, no. 6 (1983): 1119–23.

7. Judith Sharlin and Sari Edelstein, *Essentials of Life Cycle Nutrition* (Sudbury: Jones and Barlett Publishers; 2011): 36.

8. Arthur I. Eidelman and Richard J. Schanler, "Breastfeeding and the Use of Human Milk," *Pediatrics* 129, (2012):829–41, http://pediatrics.aappublications.org/content/129/3/e827.full.html.

9. Laurence M. Grummer-Strawn, Kelly S. Scanlon and Sara B. Fein, "Infant Feeding and Feeding Transitions During the First Year of Life," *Pediatrics* 122 (2008): s36–s42.

10. "Introducing Solid Foods to Toddlers," Reviewed 2012, *The Academy of Nutrition and Dietetics* http://www.eatright.org/Public/content.aspx?id=8049.

11. "Guidelines for the Diagnosis and Management of Food Allergy in the United States," *National Institute of Health*, No. 11–7700 (2010), http://www.niaid.nih.gov/topics/foodallergy/clinical/pages/default.aspx.

12. Lena Davidsson, Peter Kastenmayer, Hanna Szajewska, Richard F. Hurrell and Denis Barclay, "Iron Bioavailability in Infants from an Infant Cereal Fortified with Ferric Pyrophospate or Ferrous Fumarate," *The American Journal of Clinical Nutrition*. 71, (2000): 1597–1602.

13. Nancy Butte, Kathleen Cobb, Johanna Dwyer, Laura Graney, William Heird and Karyl Richard, "The Start Healthy Feeding Guidelines for Infants and Toddlers," *The American Dietetic Association* 104, no. 3 (2004): 442–54.

14. Nancy F. Krebs, Jamie E. Westcott, Nancy Butler, Cordelia Robinson, Melanie Bell, and K. Michael Hambidge, "Meat as a First Complementary Food for Breastfed Infants: Feasibility and Impact on Zinc Intake and Status," *Journal of Pediatric Gastroenterology and Nutrition* 42, no. 2 (2006): 207–14. Http://journals.lww.com/jpgn/Abstract/2006/02000/Meat_as_a_First_Complementary_Food_for_Breastfed.18.aspx.

15. "Arsenic in Your Food: Our Findings Show a Real Need for Federal Standards for This Toxin," November 2012.

16. Laurence M. Grummer-Strawn, Kelly S. Scanlon and Sara B. Fein, "Infant Feeding and Feeding Transitions During the First Year of Life," *Pediatrics* 122 (2008): s36–s42.

17. Nancy F. Krebs, Jamie E. Westcott, Nancy Butler, Cordelia Robinson, Melanie Bell, and K. Michael Hambidge, "Meat as a First Complementary Food for Breastfed Infants: Feasibility and Impact on Zinc Intake and Status," *Journal of Pediatric Gastroenterology and Nutrition* 42, no. 2 (2006): 207–14. http://journals.lww.com/jpgn/Abstract/2006/02000/Meat_as_a_First_Complementary_Food_for_Breastfed.18.aspx.

18. Sanju Jalla, Jamie Westcott, Marsha Steirn, Leland Miller, Melanie Bell, and Nancy Krebs, "Zinc Absorption and Exchangeable Zinc Pool Sizes in Breast-Fed Infants Fed Meat or Cereal as First Complementary Food" *Journal of Pediatric Gastroenterology and Nutrition* 34, no. 1 (2002): 35–41.

19. MD Engelmann, L. Davidsson, B Sandstrom, T. Walczyk, RF Hurrell, and KF Michaelsen, "The Influence of Meat on Nonheme Iron Absorption in Infants." *Pediatric Research*, 43 (1998): 768–73. Http://consumerreports.org/cro/magazine/2012/11/arsenic-in-your-food/index.htm.

20. Judith E. Brown, *Nutrition Through the Life Cycle* , 5th ed. (Stamford: Cengage Learning, 2014), 240.

21. Judith Sharlin and Sari Edelstein, *Essentials of Life Cycle Nutrition* (Sudbury: Jones and Bartlett Publishers; 2011): 42–43.

22. Nancy Butte, Kathleen Cobb, Johanna Dwyer, Laura Graney, William Heird, and Karyl Rickard, "The Start Healthy Feeding Guidelines for Infants and Toddlers," *The American Dietetic Association* 104, no. 3 (2004): 442–54.

23. Patricia Queen Samour and Kathy King, *Handbook of Pediatric Nutrition* 3rd Ed. (Sudbury: Jones and Bartlett Publishers, 2005), 112.

24. Judith Sharlin and Sari Edelstein, *Essentials of Life Cycle Nutrition*, (Sudbury: Jones and Bartlett Publishers), 43.

25. Ronette R. Briefel, Kathleen Reidy, Vatsala Karwe, and Barbara Devaney, "Feeding Infants and Toddlers Study: Improvements Needed in Meeting Infant Feeding Recommendations," *Journal of The American Dietetic Association* 104, no. 1 (2004): s31–s37.

26. Susan A. Sullivan and Leann L. Birch, "Infant Dietary Experience and Acceptance of Solid Foods," *Pediatrics* 93, no. 2 (1994): 271–77.

27. AK. Ventura and J. Worobey, "Early Influences on the Development of Food Preferences," *Current Biology*. 23, no. 9 (2013): R401–8.

28. Suzanne Evans Morris and Marsha Dunn Klein, *Pre-Feeding Skills 2nd Ed.* (Austin Pro-ed, 2000), 525.

29. Betty Ruth Carruth, Paula J. Ziegler, Anne Gordon, and Kristy Hendricks, "Developmental Milestones and Self-Feeding Behaviors in Infants and Toddlers," *The American Dietetic Association* 104, no. 1 (2004): s51–s56.

30. Ellen Townsend and Nicola J. Pitchford, "Baby Knows Best? The Impact of Weaning Style on Food Preferences and Body Mass Index in Early Childhood in a Case-controlled Sample," *BMJ Open* 2, (2012): 1–6.

31. Robert A. Wood, "The Natural History of Food Allergy," *Pediatrics* 111, no. 6 (2003): 1631–36.

32. Caroline Wellbery, "Optimal Time to Initiate Cereal Exposure in Infants," *American Family Physician* 69, no. 8 (2004): 2006–2007.

33. Du G. Toit, Y. Katz, P. Sasieni, et al, "Early Consumption of Peanuts in Infancy is Associated with a Low Prevalence of Peanut Allergy," *Pediatrics* 124, no. 2 (2009): s118–s119.

34. "Guidelines for the Diagnosis and Management of Food Allergy in the United States," *National Institutes of Health*, No. 11–7700 (2010).

35. Sally Fallon Morell and Thomas S. Cowan, *The Nourishing Traditions Book of Baby & Child Care*, (Washington: New Trends Publishing, 2013) 196.

36. Anneli Ivarsson, Anna Myléus, Fredrik Norström, Maria van der Pals, Anna Rosén, Lotta Högberg, Lars Danielsson, Britta Halvarsson, Solveig Hammarroth, Olle Hernell, Eva Karlsson, Lars Stenhammar, Charlotta Webb, Olof Sandstrom, and Annelie Carlsson. "Prevalence of Childhood Celiac Disease and Changes in Infant Feeding." *Pediatrics*. 131, 3 (2013): e687–e694.

37. "Joint Statement: Timing of Introduction of Gluten Into the Infant Diet" (2011) http://cot.food.gov.uk/cotstatements/cotstatementsyrs/cotstatements2011/cot201101.

38. Dietary Guidelines Advisory Committee, "Report of the Dietary Guidelines Advisory Committee on the Dietary Guidelines for Americans, 2010, to the Secretary of Agriculture and the Secretary of Health and Human Services," Washington, DC: US Department of Agriculture, Agricultural Research Service. http://www.cnpp.usda/gov/DGAs2010-DGACReprot.htm.

39. Louise A. Berner, Debra R. Keast, Regan L. Bailey, and Johanna T. Dwyer, "Fortified Foods Are Major Contributors to Nutrient Intakes in Diets of US Children and Adolescents," *Journal of the Academy of Nutrition and Dietetics*, (2014): 1–14.

Chapter 4

Nourishing Foods for the First Year and Beyond

Nourishing Proteins

Proteins (animal and plant sources) are vital to all cells in the human body. In other words, protein is found everywhere in the body. Keeping us together "structurally," they are essential for growth, tissue repair, and energy. Other functions include transporting vitamins and minerals throughout the body, building a strong immune system, and maintaining our water balance.

Animal protein sources include meat, poultry, pork, fish, eggs, and dairy. Animal sources of protein are considered complete because they contain all of the amino acids (building blocks of protein) in the amounts the body needs. Proteins from animal sources are also easily digested in the human body.

Plant protein sources such as beans, lentils, vegetables, grains, nuts, and seeds are referred to as incomplete proteins. An incomplete protein lacks one or more essential amino acids. The good news is that high protein plant foods such as lentils, dried beans, and peas, contribute to an increase in fiber, vitamins, and minerals. If you choose a vegetarian lifestyle, consider eating protein foods that complete each other. A complete protein food combination provides the amino acids the combining food lacks.

Common Complementary Food Combinations

- Beans and grains (quinoa, millet, rice)
- Beans with tortillas
- Rice with lentils
- Pea soup with crackers
- Hummus with sesame paste
- Pasta with beans
- Nut butter with bread
- Macaroni and cheese

So how much protein does your little one need? Up to six months of age, breast milk and formula provide the infant with adequate protein. After six months, solid food will provide additional protein intake. The current recommendation for children between the ages of one and three is approximately 10% to 20% of total food calories from protein. This range ensures that enough energy is provided to the body from other nutrients so that the protein can do its job and can be used for growth and development.

Nourishing Carbohydrates

Carbohydrates are the main source of energy for the human body. There are two types of carbohydrates: simple and complex. Simple carbohydrates include sugar, honey, corn syrup, and maple syrup. They are digested very fast and contribute to very few nutrients in the diet. Starch and fiber are considered complex carbohydrates. They take longer to digest and provide the body with vitamins and minerals. Complex carbohydrates come from milk, yogurt, and plant foods—including fruits, vegetables, legumes, and whole grains.

At this time, there isn't a formal recommendation for infant and toddler carbohydrate intake. Eating a variety of fruits, vegetables, beans, and grains will provide the balance of nutrients needed for healthy growth and development. When shopping, look for products that are made with whole grains. Avoid refined grains as much as possible. It is important to limit simple sugar foods and beverages (candy, juice, cake, and so on) to special occasions.

Nourishing Fats and a Healthy Brain

Fat, unfortunately, is one of the most misunderstood nutrients. In today's fat-frightened world, we are fast to buy the skim milk, avoid eggs, and grill lean meats. Fat is packed with the most calories per gram, offering a great source of energy. Fat also insulates the body and protects delicate organs. Fat aids in the digestion, absorption, and metabolism of all fat-soluble vitamins—A, D, E, and K. Fats also contribute a sensory quality to our food. They provide flavor and texture, giving us a great sense of pleasure as we eat. Even if you are on a fat-free or low-fat diet, infants and children should not be. If you are planning a family meal, participate in the meal but add more vegetables and fruits to your plate.

Fats are vital to the growth of your baby. I am including saturated fat and cholesterol—not just omega-3 fatty acids. In the first two years of life, an infant's brain will triple in size. Let me repeat: Your baby's brain and body are going to grow rapidly in the next two years. Choosing the right types of fats is important to the development of your child. Trans fats (hydrogenated oils) should be avoided, while the fats found in avocados, coconut, olives, nuts, seeds, pastured animals, and small oily fish should be considered as a source of fat for your infant. Aim for approximately 30% of total calories to come from fat.[1–3]

Healthy Fat Type	Food Sources	Function
Alpha-Linolenic Acid (omega-3)	Breast milk, flax seed, hemp seed, pumpkin, chia, walnuts, green leafy vegetables, pastured animal products	Must be present for the body to make its own DHA (not an efficient process).
EPA (omega-3)	Breast milk, Atlantic mackerel, sardines, wild salmon, algae, pastured animal products	A critical fatty acid found throughout the body which influences immunity and blood supply to the brain.
DHA (omega-3)	Breast milk, Atlantic mackerel, sardines, wild salmon, algae, pastured animal products	A critical fatty acid found in the brain.

Healthy Fat = Healthy Brain

The human brain is constructed of mostly fat with omega-3 fatty acids (DHA and EPA), creating the architecture and structure of the brain. DHA and EPA are to brain development what calcium is to bone growth. In fact, DHA continues to build up in the brain until the age of two. The brain predominately relies on saturated fat, cholesterol, and polyunsaturated fat for growth. Fortunately for us, our body has the ability to make saturated fat, cholesterol, and some polyunsaturated fats. However, there are two polyunsaturated fats (EPA and DHA) that must be obtained from our diet. While our bodies can make them, it is a very inefficient process. Low intake levels of DHA during pregnancy, breastfeeding, and self-feeding have been associated with lower IQ, an increased risk of sudden infant death syndrome (SIDS), decreased hand-eye coordination, and an increased risk of chronic disease.[4–7]

Nourishing Vitamins and Minerals

Vitamins and minerals perform a wide variety of functions in the body. See the chart of vitamins and minerals on pages 57–58. Typically, healthy children do not need a supplement of vitamins and minerals if they eat a balanced diet of fat, protein, and carbohydrates, full of a colorful variety of fruits and vegetables. If you do give your child supplements, please do so under medical supervision. Supplemental vitamins and minerals taken in excess can cause harm and, even worse, death.

In the United States, there are vitamin and mineral deficiencies of concern for the growing child. As discussed on pages 36–37, beginning at six months of age an infant could be at risk for iron, zinc, vitamin D, and omega-3 fatty acids deficiencies. In order to meet their needs, we need to provide our children with a balanced diet. Unfortunately, minerals in general can be hard to digest. Pairing foods in meal preparation can either increase or decrease the success rate of mineral absorption. For example, foods high in iron are better absorbed if served with a vitamin C rich food.[8] But when iron intake is accompanied with a high calcium, phytate, or oxalate intake (see page 59 for more information), the absorption rate of iron is decreased. Don't let this scare you; eating a variety of foods will provide a balance of nutrition. However, I will take it a step further, ensuring maximum absorption of nutrients in the recipes found at the end of this book.

Nourishing Foods for Dense Bones, Powerful Brains, Tough Immunities, and Strong Muscles

Vitamins	Sources	Function
A	Breast milk, pastured organic liver, pastured butter, pastured egg yolks, whole-fat pastured dairy, wild-caught fish, cod liver oil Beta-carotene (vitamin A precursor): breast milk, formula, carrots, red peppers, pumpkin, sweet potatoes, peas, tomatoes, apricots, mango, watermelon, collards, spinach, broccoli	Antioxidant, vision, cell production, cell growth (maturation of stem cells), turnover of epithelial tissue (skin, mucous membranes and other lining materials in the body), immune function, reproduction and growth of bone cells
D	Breast milk, formula, sunlight, pastured butter, pastured egg yolks, whole-fat pastured dairy, sardines, wild salmon, tuna, cheese, pastured meats, pastured organ meats, cod liver oil	Regulates blood calcium levels
E	Breast milk, formula, pastured butter, avocados, nuts, wheat germ, pastured eggs	Antioxidant, protects lipids in cell membranes
K	Breast milk, formula, pastured egg yolks, green leafy vegetables, cabbage, broccoli, potatoes, oats	Blood clotting, bone formation
C	Breast milk, formula, citrus, berries, papaya, parsley, kiwi, dark green leafy veggies, broccoli, plums, cherries, peaches, apples, pears, nectarines, melon, pineapple, grapes, asparagus, basil, sweet peppers, mango, potato skins (purée or dice finely to prevent choking hazard)	Antioxidant, collagen synthesis, immune function
B	Breast milk, formula, pastured egg yolks, pastured meat products, whole-fat pastured dairy, wild-caught fish, clams, pastured beef and chicken liver, leafy greens, nuts, seeds, soaked beans, vegetables, grain products	Energy production, immune function, lowers homocysteine (amino acid associated with heart disease), DNA synthesis, nerve cell maintenance
Choline (vitamin-like substance)	Breast milk, pastured egg yolks, pastured meat products, whole-fat pastured dairy, pastured organic liver, peanuts	Lowers homocysteine, protects cell membranes, maintains cell's shape, enables fatty substances to mix with water

Minerals	Sources	Function
Calcium	Breast milk, formula, whole pastured dairy, cheese, sardines, sesame seeds, leafy greens, parsley, basil, wild salmon, nuts, pinto beans, dried figs	Muscle contraction, nerve impulse transmission, blood clotting, cell metabolism
Iodine	Breast milk, formula, pastured eggs, wild-caught cod, pastured beef liver, navy beans, potatoes, pastured poultry, kelp	Thyroid function: regulates body temperature, basal metabolic rate, reproduction, growth
Iron	Breast milk, formula, pastured organic liver, pastured meat, pastured egg yolks, oily fish, kelp, lentils, green leafy vegetables, raisins, prunes, avocado, peas, spinach, dried apricots, unsulfured blackstrap molasses, clams, nuts	Oxygen transport, energy production, amino acid metabolism, muscle function, immune function, brain function, nervous system development
Maganese	Breast milk, formula, nuts, whole grain, tea	Energy production, builds cartilage, anti-oxidant, and urea formation
Magnesium	Breast milk, formula, sesame seeds, halibut, almonds, cashews, soaked black beans, whole wheat, dried fruit, bananas, leafy green vegetables	DNA and protein synthesis, blood clotting, muscle contraction, energy production
Potassium	Breast milk, formula, banana, potato skins, cantaloupe, plain yogurt, tomato juice, clams, halibut, spinach, apricot, pastured milk, acorn squash	Muscle contractions, transmits nerve impulses, regulates blood pressure and heartbeat
Selenium	Breast milk, formula, brazil nuts, pastured beef liver, pork, pastured eggs, cottage cheese, oatmeal	Thyroid function, antioxidant, immune function
Potassium	Breast milk, formula, pastured meat, pastured organic liver, sardines, pastured eggs, pastured dark meat poultry, oysters, crab, garlic, nuts, dark green leafy vegetables, cheese, lentils, split peas, lima beans, peas, parsley, red meat, peanuts, pumpkin seeds, sunflower seeds	Helps (cofactor) in nearly 100 enzymes in the body, gene expression, cell death, nerve transmission

The Anti-Nutrients

Oxalate, Phytate, Goitrogens, and Solanine

If you have been on the raw diet or involved in the green smoothie movement, or you at least follow them on social media, you might recognize some of these words: oxalate, phytate, goitrogens, and solanine. Oxalate is found in leafy greens and naturally binds calcium, decreasing its absorption rate. The biggest offenders are rhubarb (500+mg per ½ cup) and spinach (700+ mg per ½ cup cooked). While kale is in the low oxalate category (2 mg per 1 cup raw) it always seems to get lumped into the high oxalate category by default—after all, it is a leafy green—but that does not make it high in oxalate. Surprisingly, it is extremely low in oxalate acid. In fact, one banana has more oxalate than 1 cup of kale![9–10]

Phytate is a compound found in whole grains and legumes. It binds minerals, making them non-digestible, which sets us up for bone loss and other diseases. We want our children to absorb minerals such as iron, zinc, magnesium, selenium, and calcium. In order to reduce phytate in legumes, it is important to soak them for 24 hours before cooking.[11–12]

The word "goitrogen" is not as popular, but if you follow the raw diet trends, you might have heard of it. Goitrogens are compounds found in vegetables of the cabbage family: broccoli, cauliflower, brussels sprouts, and cabbage (for the most part). Goitrogens

can cause an iodine deficiency because they decrease the body's absorption of iodine. The good news is that cooking your vegetables inactivates goitrogens.[13]

Last but not least—solanine. Solanine is a toxic alkaloid (nitrogenous organic compound of plant origin that is toxic to humans). It is the greenish color found under potato skins. Don't worry—not all potatoes have this compound.

It is only present if you see green between the skin and flesh of the potato. You can remove it by peeling the potato or buying potatoes without the green coloring. If you continue to see green as you peel the potato, you may want to toss it in the garbage or compost.[14]

Organic

What does it really mean?

Some health professionals say that eating organic is a lifestyle, but I believe it is a choice. It is your right to be informed and to make the best possible decisions for your family. Organic food is grown and produced according to a set of standards established by the U.S. Department of Agriculture (USDA). Organic foods are theoretically free of:

- High fructose corn syrup
- Artificial colorings and sweeteners
- Growth hormones
- Synthetic chemicals—fertilizers and pesticides, herbicides, and fungicides

There is growing evidence that synthetic chemicals used in conventional food production have a negative impact on fetuses, infants, and children (brain damage, impaired immune systems, autism, eczema, infectious diseases, behavioral problems, and lower IQ).[15–20] Infants and children are more

sensitive to the effects of pesticide residues because they have a small body size. Children are still developing vital organs and lack the enzymes needed to aid the detoxification of neurotoxic (bad for the brain) chemicals. If you think about it, children consume more food per pound of body weight compared to adults to keep up with their fast rate of growth. Organic food consumption does reduce the exposure to synthetic chemicals.[21–26]

Organic and conventional foods are currently battling for the honor of containing the most nutrients per serving.[27–29] Even if conventional foods have just as much nutrition (vitamins, minerals, fat, protein, carbohydrates, and calories) as organic foods, they are not necessarily equal. Yes, food gives us our source of vital minerals and vitamins, but it can also be a delivery vehicle for harmful chemicals and toxins.

Organic produce is expensive and, if you cannot afford to be 100% organic, do not beat yourself up. Let me be honest here: I do not eat 100% organic. It is hard and, quite frankly, almost impossible to do.

I do not want to create "mom guilt" among my readers. We have too many things to worry about. My advice? Start small and take baby steps. We can only do so much, but you have the power to make decisions. You are already ahead of the game by investing the time to teach taste, encourage self-feeding, and offer a variety of nutrient-rich foods. The good news is that organic foods are popping up all over the place (Walmart, bulk buying clubs, Target, and so on), making them more affordable than ever.

If organic foods are too pricey for your wallet, don't stop eating fruits and vegetables to

avoid synthetic chemical exposure. The nutritional benefits of produce outweigh the risk of synthetic chemicals. Produce, especially a variety, will provide you with the nutrients and phytochemicals needed to defend against disease and infection. Each year, the Environmental Working Group ranks produce by its pesticide content, and compiles a list called the "dirty dozen." This list is a great reference, if your budget does not allow a 100% organic diet. This list changes each year, so make sure you get the most up-to-date list online. Currently the "dirty dozen" list includes:

- Apples
- Bell peppers
- Blueberries
- Celery
- Cucumbers
- Grapes
- Lettuce
- Nectarines
- Peaches
- Potatoes
- Strawberries
- Spinach

Pastured Animals vs. Commercially Raised Animals

Organic meat limits your exposure to hormones and disease resistant antibiotics, but it does not necessarily increase the nutrient content of the meat, poultry, or eggs. Animals that graze daily on grass and feel the sun on their backs are a better food for us.

Pastured animals store more vitamin D, vitamin A, vitamin E, conjugated linoleic acid, and omega-3 fatty acids in their fat.[30–31]

Currently, animals in conventional feedlots are raised on a diet of corn, soy, and feedstuff. Feedstuff consumption in cattle increases as corn prices increase, which is caused by droughts and other poor weather conditions. Feedstuff includes anything from candy, gum with wrappers, "chicken litter" (stuff from the floor of chicken coops), cardboard, municipal garbage, and other processed foods.[32] Even worse, animals in conventional feedlots may never feel the sun, graze in a pasture, or get appropriate exercise.

Yes, I know, pastured animal products are expensive. Again, start small and make a couple changes. Visit your local farmers and ask them questions. If they cannot tell you what they feed their animals or whether their animals live outside on some or most days, do not trust their product. When I transitioned from conventionally raised animal protein to local pastured animal products, I started with eggs and cheaper cuts of meat (whole chickens, chicken thighs, ground beef, ground bison).

To eat pastured animals within my budget, I decreased the amount of animal protein my family consumed, but increased the quality of it. Yes, I will spend close to twenty dollars on one chicken, but I create two to four meals from that chicken, extending the product and maximizing nutrient intake. If you buy one whole chicken, you can make a couple of the following recipes in this book: Toddler's Chicken Salad, Real Food Chicken Tenders, Chicken Pot Pie, Cornbread Dressing Cakes, Southwestern Burrito Baby, Asian Burrito Baby, and Bone Broth.

Top 10 Cost-Saving Tips to Eat Pastured Animal Products

- Use pastured butter and eggs. They are cheaper animal products, packed with loads of nutrients.
- Decrease the amount of animal products you consume weekly, but increase the quality.
- Use pastured meat products as flavoring in casseroles, stews, and soups. In other words, make multiple meals out of one free-range product (using bones, fat, and meat).
- Increase the amount of vegetables in each dish or meal you make.
- Buy a whole chicken and butcher the meat yourself.
- Use a cheaper cut of meat (chicken thighs with bone and skin).
- Stock up when meat is on sale.
- Invest in a freezer and buy in bulk.
- Use all parts of the animal (bone for soup, skin for fat and flavoring, organs for sweet breads).
- Start slow. If there is something your family always consumes, focus on purchasing that product pastured.

Cost Saving Tips to Reduce Chemical Overload

- Refer to the Environmental Working Group's "Shopper's Guide to Pesticides" at www.foodnews.org, and this Consumer Reports article from 2008 at www.consumerreports.org/health/healthy-living/diet-nutrition/healthy-foods/organic-foods/overview/when-to-buy-organic.htm.
- If there is a produce item you consume a lot of, commit to purchasing that specific item organic.
- Buy frozen organic local produce.
- Visit your local farmer's market and buy local produce from a local farm with many different crops.
- Buy produce in season.
- Start small, growing produce around your house or in window boxes (edible landscaping).
- Buy products free of high fructose corn syrup.
- Look for food items that use natural food colorings such as beet juice powder, and that are free of artificial colorings.
- Purchase organic products in bulk.
- Add variety to your produce; don't eat the same thing all the time.

from the mom tip

"Because of the cost of organic meat I tend to recommend to clients (and choose for my family) locally produced meat but not necessarily organic. It is important for me to know where my food comes from."

–Liz RD, CDE Burlington, VT

Beyond Nutrition

The "Other" Stuff in Food

Child development is a fragile progression, involving not only how we feed our children, but what we feed our children. Food and nutrition are vital to overall health. I am not just talking about vitamins, minerals, protein, fiber, and omega-3 fatty acids (all the good stuff we tend to concentrate on). I am also talking about the other stuff riddled in our commercial food supply.

To be honest, seven years ago, I really did not care about personal nutrition, food additives, organic food, pesticides, and everything else I am failing to mention, until I decided to have children. Having children gave me a greater sense of myself. I changed my view of the world. Suddenly, life had new meaning; I was living and breathing for someone else—a feeling parents can deeply understand. My renewed sense of self wanted to protect this little human with all of my energy and resources. I wanted to learn everything about raising a healthy child. I wanted my child to thrive—not just survive—and this meant learning more about nutrition than I had formally studied.

Many of the topics listed below are not only controversial, but are in need of more research. As a mother, if something could be considered harmful or even questionable, I would not wait twenty more years for research to tell me I should have avoided it in the first place. So yes, I do urge you to learn as much as you can and stay up-to-date with the latest research. And yes, as a mother, I am going to tell you to limit the additives and food processing procedures listed below, to err on the side of safety and health for your child. I do. I am not perfect, and I am not 100% chemical free. It is an impossible feat, but you can take measures to limit these potentially harmful substances—knowledge is power.

Honey

This is not controversial. It is well known that an infant should avoid honey in the first year of life. Honey can cause infant botulism. Botulism is a rare but very serious food poisoning. After the age of one, it is okay to feed your child recipes with honey, which is a common sugar substitute in this book.

Fruit Juices

The American Academy of Pediatrics recommends that fruit juice intake be limited to 4–6 ounces per day. Excessive juice consumption has been linked to poor health. Juice intake prior to a meal can fill up a little belly, causing a decrease in appetite and food refusal. Chronic juice consumption may displace nutrients from a meal, causing failure to thrive or malnutrition.[33]

High Fructose Corn Syrup (HFCS)

HFCS is a common form of sugar, used in processed foods because it is cheap and it increases the shelf-life of products. However, it is not as sweet as it sounds. HFCS has been linked to obesity, diabetes, attention-deficient disorders, and cardiovascular disease. It has also been associated with mineral imbalances and high levels of mercury. The good news is that companies are starting to remove it from their products. HFCS should be avoided.[34–37]

Trans-Fats

Trans-fats should be avoided at all costs, due the recent research associating them with poor heart health. Trans-fats are found in most processed foods and margarine in the form of hydrogenated or partially hydrogenated oils. They are added to food to increase shelf-life, increase texture, and decrease cost.

Nitrates

Nitrates are found in commercially processed meats, like hot dogs, lunch meats, bacon, and ham. Nitrates have been associated with an increase in cancer and methemoglobinemia (nitrate poisoning). Nitrates are added to prevent the growth of bad bacteria and to enhance the color of meat.

Unfortunately, nitrates are naturally found in water and are also commonly used in fertilizers. They are hard to avoid, and buying organic does not eliminate them totally. Vegetables high in nitrates include: spinach, carrots, green beans, squash, broccoli, and beets. These foods should be avoided in children younger than three months of age. After the first three months, the baby's red blood cells are more mature and can handle the exposure of nitrate in food. If you are formula-feeding and use well water, have your water tested for nitrate concentration, or use filtered water. The federal contaminant level is 10 ppm (parts per million) nitrate nitrogen.[38–39]

Food Colorings

Artificial food colorings are commonly added to our commercial food supply, making food more appealing to the consumer. Unfortunately, artificial food colorings have been linked to hyperactivity, behavioral issues, and zinc deficiency. Zinc is not only a vital mineral, but is instrumental in eliminating mercury (a toxin) from the body. As a mother, I look for foods colored with beet powder and other natural colorings.[40–43]

Artificial Sweeteners

Controversy has surrounded artificial sweeteners since their discovery. Research has been conflicting regarding their impact on diseases like cancer, Parkinson's, Alzheimer's, multiple sclerosis, autism, and lupus.[44] It is not worth the risk. Artificial sweeteners should be avoided, especially in children.

Endocrine Disruptors

Endocrine disruptors, also known as environmental toxins, are hormone-altering chemicals that have been associated with a long list of diseases including cancer, behavioral issues, early puberty, diabetes, kidney damage, reproductive problems, and brain damage.[45–51] Fetuses, infants, and children are particularly vulnerable to the exposure of environmental toxins because they are developing at critical points in their life. The following three practices have been identified to help lower exposure to environmental toxins: eat organic or homegrown foods without chemicals, limit the use of personal care products (no warning label), and avoid the use of plastic.[52–54]

BPA and Phthalates

Bisphenol A (BPA) and phthalates are toxic chemical building bocks used in the manufacturing of plastics. They are commonly found in plastic food containers and plastic wraps. If you are using a plastic container or plastic wrap for food, BPA and phthalates will leach into the food or beverage—especially when the food contains fat or is heated. To avoid these toxic chemicals, use stainless steel, wax paper, or glass whenever possible. Phthalates are also used to make plastic (toys, shower curtains, vinyl flooring), personal care products, and wood finishers. Think before you use personal care products. If there is a warning label on your baby lotion or shampoo, you may want to rethink putting it on your baby's skin. Olive and nut oils make great skin moisturizers and add nutrition along the way.

Lead

Lead is found in lead-based paints, old housing pipes, and water. Using a water filter in your home will decrease lead exposure. If you live in an older home, run your faucet water for 30 seconds to clean out any stale water in the pipes. As water sits in the pipe, it absorbs the iron. Eating a diet high in fruits and vegetables will decrease the absorption rate and increase the excretion of lead.

Arsenic

Arsenic naturally shows up in our food and water supply because it lives in the soil. Unfortunately, organic and conventionally grown foods have the same levels of arsenic. The biggest food of concern for infants is infant rice cereal. According to Consumer Reports, rice has a higher concentration of arsenic than other grains such as oats. The cumulative impact of exposure to rice—even at low concentrations—can be harmful to pregnant women and infants. To reduce arsenic exposure:

- Use other grain infant or homemade cereals such as oatmeal and barley.
- Use a variety of grains in family meals: quinoa, barley, polenta, couscous, or bulgur wheat.
- Soak and rinse rice prior to cooking.
- Cook rice in 6 times more water to reduce up to half of the arsenic content, making it more comparable to the concentration found in oatmeal.
- Clean vegetable skins thoroughly before cooking or eating.
- Avoid apple and grape juice consumption, which is also high in arsenic.
- Invest in a good water filter. To find a water filter, check out www.ewg.org/report/ewgs-water-filter-buying-guide.[55–57]

Mercury

According to the American Academy of Pediatrics, all forms of mercury should be minimized for optimal growth and development of infants and children, because it has a negative impact on growth and brain development.[58] Mercury does occur naturally in our food, but it can be consumed in toxic amounts.

Food sources of mercury include larger fish (shark, swordfish, tuna) and high fructose corn syrup (HFCS). Although the sample size in the HFCS study was small, The Environmental Health published an executive summary stating, "HFCS now appears to be a significant additional source of mercury." HFCS is found in the majority of processed foods like yogurt, juice, soda, nutrition bars, cereals, and baked goods. To limit mercury consumption, eat small wild fish that feed on algae and other smaller fish (Atlantic mackerel, haddock, wild salmon) and avoid HFCS.[59–60]

Chapter 4 References

1. J.M. Bourre, "Effects of Nutrients (In Food) on the Structure and Function of the Nervous System: Update on Dietary Requirements for Brain. Part 2: Macronutrients," *The Journal of Nutrition, Health & Aging,* 10 (2006): 386–97.

2. Michael A. Schmidt, *Brain-Building Nutrition* 3rd Edition, (Berkeley: North Atlantic Books, 2007), 132.

3. Dimitri Christakis, "Media and Children," *TEDxRainer*, December 27, 2011. http://www.youtube.com/watch?v=BoT7qH_uVNo.

4. Liz Wolfe, *Eat the Yolks* (Las Vegas: Victory Belt Publishing, 2013), 223–36.

5. Evelyn Tribole, *The Ultimate Omega-3 Diet* (New York: McGraw Hill, 2007), 90–93.

6. Ibid.

7. Michael A. Schmidt, *Brain-Building Nutrition 3rd Ed.* (Berkeley: North Atlantic Books, 2007), 47.

8. E.R. Monsen, "Iron Nutrition and Absorption: Dietary Factors which Impact Iron Bioavailability," *Journal of the American Dietetic Association*. 88, no. 7 (1988): 786–90.

9. Paul Insel, Don Ross, Kimberley McMahon, and Melissa Bernstein, *Discovering Nutrition 4th Ed.* (Burlington: Jones & Bartlett Learning, 2013): 395.

10. "Oxalate Content of Foods," *Harvard School of Public Health*, 2008 https://regepi.bwh.harvard.edu/health/Oxalate/files.

11. Paul Insel, Don Ross, Kimberley McMahon, and Melissa Bernstein, *Discovering Nutrition 4th Ed.* (Burlington: Jones & Bartlett Learning, 2013): 395.

12. "Living with Phytic Acid," *The Weston A. Price Foundation*, March 26, 2010, http://www.westonaprice.org/food-features/living-with-phytic-acid.

13. Paul Insel, Don Ross, Kimberley McMahon, and Melissa Bernstein, *Discovering Nutrition 4th Ed.* (Burlington: Jones & Bartlett Learning, 2013): 421.

14. Paul Insel, Don Ross, Kimberley McMahon, and Melissa Bernstein, *Discovering Nutrition 4th Ed.* (Burlington: Jones & Bartlett Learning, 2013): 585.

15. Joseph L. Jacobson and Sandra W. Jacobson, "Intellectual Impairment in Children Exposed to Polychlorinated Biphenyls in Utero," *The New England Journal of Medicine* 335, no. 11 (1996): 783–89.

16. Virginia Rauh, Srikesh Arunajadai, Megan Horton, Frederica Perera, Lori Hoepner, Dana B. Barr, and Robin Whyatt, "Seven-Year Neurodevelopmental Scores and Prenatal Exposure to Chlorpyrifos, a Common Agricultural Pesticide," *Environmental Health Perspectives* 119, no. 8 (2011): 1196–1201.

17. Maryse F. Bouchard, David C. Bellinger, Robert O. Wright, and Marc G. Weisskopf, "Attention-Deficit/Hyperactivity Disorder and Urinary Metabolites of Organophosphate Pesticides," *Pediatrics* 125, no. 6 (2010): e1270–e1277.

18. "Organophosphate Insecticides in Children's Food" *The Environmental Working Group* (1998) http://www.ewg.org/research/overexposed-organophosphate-insecticides-childrens-food.

19. Maryse F. Bouchard, Jonathan Chevrier, Kim G. Harley, Katherine Kogut, Michelle Vedar, Norma Calderon, Celina Trujillo, Carolin Johnson, Asa Bradman, Dana Boyd Barr, and Brenda Eskenazi, "Prenatal Exposure to Organophosphate Pesticides and IQ in 7-Year-Old Children," *Environmental Health Perspectives* 119, no. 8 (2011): 1189–95.

20. Charles Benbrook, "Initial Reflections on the Annals of Internal Medicine Paper 'Are Organic Foods Safer and Healthier than Conventional Alternatives? A Systematic Review'," *Center for Sustaining Agriculture and Natural Resources* (2012): 1–12.

21 "Children Overexposed to Rocket Fuel Chemical," *Environmental Working Group*, October 25, 2007, http://www.ewg.org/research/children-overexposed-rocket-fuel-chemical.

22. Chensheng Lu, Dana B. Barr, and Lance A. Waller, "Dietary Intake and its Contribution to Longitudinal Organophosphorus Pesticide Exposure in Urban/Suburban Children," *Environmental Health Perspective*, 116 no. 4 (2008): 537–542, National Institutes of Health http://www.ncbi.nlm.nih.gov/pmc/articles/PMC2290988/.

23. Maryse F. Bouchard, Jonathan Chevrier, Kim G. Harley, Katherine Kogut, Michelle Vedar, Norma Calderon, Celina Trujillo, Carolin Johnson, Asa Bradman, Dana Boyd Barr, and Brenda Eskenazi, "Prenatal Exposure to Organophosphate Pesticides and IQ in 7-Year-Old Children," *Environmental Health Perspectives* 119, no. 8 (2011): 1189–95.

24. Joel Forman and Janet Silverstein, "Organic Foods: Health and Environmental Advantages and Disadvantages," *Pediatrics* 130, (2012): e1406–e1412, http://pediatrics.aappublications.org/content/130/5/e1406.short.

25. Chensheng Lu, Dana B. Barr, and Lance A. Waller, "Dietary Intake and its Contribution to Longitudinal Organophosphorus Pesticide Exposure in Urban/Suburban Children," *Environmental Health Perspective* 116 no. 4 (2008): 537–42 National Institutes of Health, http://www.ncbi.nlm.nih.gov/pmc/articles/PMC2290988/.

26. Charles Benbrook, "Initial Reflections on the Annals of Internal Medicine Paper 'Are Organic Foods Safer and Healthier than Conventional Alternatives? A systematic Review'," *Center for Sustaining Agriculture and Natural Resources* (2012): 1–12.

27. Joel Forman and Janet Silverstein, "Organic Foods: Health and Environmental Advantages and Disadvantages." *Pediatrics* 130, (2012): e1406–e1412, http://pediatrics.aappublications.org/content/130/5/e1406.short.

28. C. Smith-Spangler, M.L. Brandeau, G.E. Hunter, J.C. Bavinger, M. Pearson, P.J. Eschbach, V. Sundaram, H. Liu, P. Schirmer, C. Stave, I. Olkin, and D.M. Bravata, "Are Organic Foods Safer or Healthier than Conventional Alternatives? A Systematic Review," *Annual Internal Medicine* 157, no. 5 (2012): 348–66.

29. Christine M. Williams, "Nutritional Quality of Organic Food: Shades of Grey or Shades of Green?" *Proceedings of the Nutrition Society* 61 (2002): 19–24.

30. Jo Robinson, *Pasture Perfect* (Vashon: Vashon Island Press, 2011), 26–29, 36.

31. S. Couvreur, C. Hurtaud, C. Lopez, L. Delaby, and J.L. Peyraud, "The Linear Relationship Between the Proportion of Fresh Grass in the Cow Diet, Milk Fatty Acid Composition, and Butter Properties" *Journal of Dairy Science* 89, no. 6 (2006): 1956–69.

32. Jo Robinson, *Pasture Perfect* (Vashon:Vashon Island Press, 2011), 24–25.

33. Patricia Queen Samour and Kathy King, *Handbook of Pediatric Nutrition 3rd Ed.* (Sudbury: Jones and Bartlett Publishers, 2005): 112, 115.

34. Vasanti S. Malik, Barry M. Popkin, George A. Bray, Jean-Pierre Despres, Walter C. Willett, and Frank B. Hu, "Sugar-Sweetened Beverages and Risk of Metabolic Syndrome and Type 2 Diabetes: A Meta-analysis," *Diabetetes Care* 33, No. 11 (2010): 2477–83, http://www.ncbi.nlm.nih.gov/pubmed/20693348.

35. C.M. Brown, AG Dulloo, and J.P. Montani, "Sugary Drinks in the Pathogenesis of Obesity and Cardiovascular Diseases," *International Journal of Obesity*, 32 (2008): s28–s34, http://www.readcube.com/articles/10.1038/ijo.2008.204.

36. Roseanne Schnoll, Dmitry Burshteyn, and Juan Cea-Aravena, "Nutrition in the Treatment of Attention-Deficit Hyperactivity Disorder: a Neglected but Important Aspect," *Applied Psychophysiology Biofeedback* 28, No.1 (2003): 63–75, http://link.springer.com/article/10.1023%2FA%3A1022321017467.

37. Renee Dufault, Roseanne Schnoll, Walter J. Lukiw, Blaise LeBlanc, Charles Cornett, Lyn Patrick, David

Wallinga, Steven G. Gilbert, and Raquel Crider, "Mercury Exposure, Nutritional Deficiencies and Metabolic Disruptions may Affect Learning in Children," *Behavioral and Brain Functions* 5, no. 44 (2009):1–15.

38. "Decoding Meat & Dairy Product Labels," 2013 *Environmental Working Group*, http://www.ewg.org/meateatersguide/decoding-meat-ddairy-product-labels/.

39. Frank R. Greer and Michael Shannon, "Infant Methe moglobinemia: The Role of Dietary Nitrate in Food and Water," *Pediatrics*, 116, no. 3 (2005): 784–86.

40. D.W. Schab and N.H. Trinh, "Do Artificial Food Colors Promote Hyperactivity in Children with Hyperactive Syndromes? A Meta-analysis of Double-blind Placebo-controlled Trials," *Journal of Developmental Behavior Pediatrics* 25, no. 6 (2004): 423–34.

41. Renee Dufault, Roseanne Schnoll, Walter J. Lukiw, Blaise LeBlanc, Charles Cornett, Lyn Patrick, David Wallinga, Steven G. Gilbert, and Raquel Crider," Mercury Exposure, Nutritional Deficiencies and Metabolic Disruptions may Affect Learning in Children," *Behavioral and Brain Functions* 5, no. 44 (2009):1–15.

42. Laura J. Stevens, Thomas Kuczek, John R. Burgess, Mateusz A. Stochelski, Eugene Arnold, and Leo Galland, "Mechanisms of Behavioral, Atopic, and other Reactions to Artificial Food colors in Children." *Nutritrion Reviews* 71, no. 5(2013): 268–81, http://onlinelibrary.wiley.com/doi/10.1111/nure.12023/abstract.

43. Renee Dufault, Roseanne Schnoll, Walter J. Lukiw, Blaise LeBlanc, Charles Cornett, Lyn Patrick, David Wallinga, Steven G. Gilbert, and Raquel Crider, "Mercury Exposure, Nutritional Deficiencies and Metabolic Disruptions may Affect Learning in Children," *Behavioral and Brain Functions* 5, no. 44 (2009): 1–15.

44. Christina R. Whitehouse, Joseph Boullata, and Linda A. McCauley, "The Potential Toxicity of Artificial Sweeteners," 56, no. 6 (2008): 251–59.

45. Whyatt R.M., Liu X, Rauh V.A., et al. "Maternal Prenatal Urinary Phthalate Metabolite Concentrations and Child Mental, Psychomotor, and Behavioral Development at 3 Years of Age," *Environmental Health Perspectives*, 120 (2012): 290–95.

46. D.T. Wigle, T.E. Arbuckle, M. Walker, M.G. Wade., S. Liu, and D. Krewski, "Environmental Hazards: Evidence for Effects on Child Health," *Journal of Toxicology Environmental Health, Part B Critical Reviews*, 10 (2007): 3–39.

47. J.M. Braun, S. Sathyanarayana, R. Hauser, "Phthalate Exposure and Children's Health," *Current Opinion in Pediatrics*, 25, no. 2 (2013): 247–54.

48 Joe M. Braun, Amy E. Kalkbrenner, Antonia M. Calafat, Kimberly Yolton, Xiaoyun Ye, Kim N. Dietrich, and Bruse P. Lanphear, "Impact of Early-Life Bisphenol A Exposure on Behavior and Executive Function in Children," *Pediatrics*, 128, no. 5 (2011): 873–82.

49. Philip Landrigan, Anjali Garg, and Daniel B.J. Droller, "Assessing the Effects of Endocrine Disruptors in the National Children's Study," *Environmental Health Perspectives*, 111, no. 13 (2003): 1678–82.

50. V. Chopra, K. Harley, M. Lahiff., and B. Eskenzai, "Association between Pthalates and Attention Deficit Disorder and Learning Disability in U.S. Children 6-15 years," *Environmental Research*, 128 (2014): 64–69.

51. Miodovnik A., Engel S.M., Zhu C., Ye X., Soorya L.V., Silva M.J., Calafat A.M., and Wolff M.S., "Endrocrine Disruptors and childhood Social Impairment," *Neurotoxicology* 32, no. 2 (2011): 261–67.

52. "Dirty Dozen List of Endocrine Disruptors," *Environmental Working Group*, 2013 http://www.ewg.org/research/dirty-dozen-list-endocrine-disruptors.

53. Camille A. Martina, Bernard Weiss, and Shanna H. Swan, "Lifestyle Behaviors Associated with Exposures to Endocrine Disruptors," *Neurotoxicology*, 33, no. 6 (2012): 1427–33.

54. R.A. Rudel, J.M Gray., C.L Engel., T.W Rawsthorn., R.E. Dodson, J.M. Ackerman, J. Rizzo, J.L. Nudelman, and J.G. Brody, "Food Packaging and Bisphenol A and Bis (2-ethyhexyl) Phthalate Exposure: Findings from a Dietary Intervention," 119, no. 7 (2011): 914–20.

55. "Questions & Answers: Arsenic in Rice and Rice Products" *FDA*, http://www.fda/gov/food/foodborneillness-contaminants/metals/ucm319948.htm.

56. "Arsenic In Your Food" *Consumer Reports* November 2012, http://consumerreports.org/cro/magazine/2012/11/arsenic-in-your-food/index.htm.

57. "Questions and Answers: Arsenic in Rice and Rice Products," *FDA*, http://www.fda.gov/Food/FoodborneIllnessContaminants/Metals/ucm319948.htm.

58. Lynn R. Goldman and Michael W. Shannon, "American Academy of Pediatrics Technical Report: Mercury In the Environment: Implications for Pediatricians," *Pediatrics* 108, no. 1 (2001): 197–205, http://pediatrics.aappublications.org/content/108/1/197.full.pdf+html.

59. Renee Dufault, Blaise LeBlanc, Roseanne Schnoll, Charles Cornett, Laura Schweitzer, David Wallinga, Jane Hightower, Lyn Patrick, and Walter J. Lukiw, "Mercury from Chlor-alkali Plants: measured Concentrations in Food Product Sugar," *Environmental Health* 8, no. 2 (2009):1–6.

60. David Wallinga, Janelle Sorensen, and Pooja Mottl, "Not So Sweet: Missing Mercury and High Fructose Corn Syrup," *Institute for Agriculture and Trade Policy*, 2009, http://www.iatp.org/documents/not-so-sweet-missing-mercury-and-high-fructose-corn-syrup.

Chapter 5

Recipes to Entice with Flavor, Texture, and Aroma

Baby Purée Basics

Babies who eat foods prepared at home have a higher acceptance rate of new foods than infants who eat commercial baby food.[1] Yes, I know. The task of making homemade baby foods sounds daunting. Especially when you can go to the store and buy ready-made baby food conveniently organized by stage of development. Allowing your baby to eat home-cooked food provides your child with more flavor, variety, and nutrients. Here is the great news—all you really need is a fork. Honestly, a fork can get the job done and you do not have to buy expensive baby food blenders, as some manufacturers will have you believe. By the time your baby is old enough to start solids (six months of age), she is old enough to eat the same food as the family. Technically, you can just mash your dinner up with a fork and thin it with breast milk or formula, if needed.

Now, let's get real here. Life happens and parents work. I do not want you to feel overwhelmed, or even worse, guilty, if you cannot make all of the food you feed your little one. If you are already over-scheduled, I recommend you make at least one meat or poultry bulk purée, and either the kale or arugula bulk purée, because you cannot buy these purées commercially.

from the mom tip

Homemade is best, with as many fruits and veggies as possible. It's worth the try!

—Melanie, Lake Placid, NY

To save time and energy, follow the recipes below using the Fast Tips for Busy Moms (page 80), or by substituting commercial baby food in the recipes where you feel fit. The good news is that you can still teach taste by adding cinnamon, ginger, rosemary, or any other flavor to commercial baby foods using the Baby Food Herb and Spice Guide on page 16. Don't forget about nature's ready-made baby foods: banana, avocado, and baked sweet potato. At minimum, you can mash up a banana, avocado, or baked sweet potato without any effort. Of course, the types of foods you serve to your infant should be determined by the existing feeding skills of your child.

Here Is What You Need:

- Blender or manual food processor (fork, food mill)
- Sauce pan (I prefer stainless steel)
- Tablespoon measuring spoon
- Chopping knife
- Thermometer
- Cutting board
- Spatula
- Glass containers with lids
- Vegetable brush
- Freezer storage tray with tablespoon-size compartments (glass deviled egg container, silicon ice cube tray, or mini-silicon cup cake pans) with covers, if possible
- Freezer
- Freezer-safe storage container
- Marker

Culinary Skills Needed:

- Boil water
- Bake and roast vegetables
- Steam vegetables and fruit
- Push a button on a blender
- Use a fork to mash
- Understand food safety
- Have fun

Benefits of Making Baby Food

- You know the food source (fresh, organic, local, frozen, etc.)
- You know what was added to the food (preservatives, food colorings, etc.)
- You have control over the allergen content (gluten, etc.)
- It tastes better
- It looks and smells better
- Pride
- It is fun!
- It is more economical

Nourishing Bulk Recipes

Batch cooking fruit and vegetable purées is a great way to be organized and have a variety of fresh food available at any given moment. The bulk recipes below are used throughout the recipes of this book. However, feel free to mix and match purées to make your own creations.

The bulk recipes can be made ahead of time and kept in the freezer for future use, saving you time, energy, and money. You will be able to grab a cube, defrost it, and serve. All of the recipes are strategically paired with other ingredients, maximizing mineral absorption to build powerful brains, dense bones, a tough immune system, and strong muscles.

Freezing and Storing Baby Food

- Prepare the bulk purées using the recipes below.
- Let the purée cool to room temperature.
- Don't worry if your purée seems too thick. You will have an opportunity to thin it before your serve it.
- Pour the purée into clean freezing trays (glass deviled egg containers) with covers. If your tray does not have a cover, use wax paper followed by plastic wrap. Do not overfill the tray as the purée may expand when frozen.
- Freeze the purée for at least 2 hours or until completely frozen.
- Remove the purée from the trays and place in a freezer-safe container with a lid.
- Label the container with the name of the food and the current date.
- Return to freezer and use within 6 months.

Preparing and Serving Baby Food

- Remove as many cubes as needed for an infant feeding.
- Defrost in the refrigerator covered, or melt in a saucepan over low heat.
- Meat, pork, and chicken should reach a temperature of 165°F.
- Prepare purée with a recipe, serve solo, or create your own fun creation by mixing and matching with other bulk purées using the Baby Herb and Spice Guide on page 16.

Oven Roasted Butternut Squash Purée

1 butternut squash or pre-diced frozen butternut squash

- Cut butternut squash in half length-wise.
- Roast flesh side-down in oven on 350°F for 30 minutes or until soft.
- Remove flesh from outer shell.
- If you have the pre-diced squash, steam over medium heat with ½ cup water until soft.
- Add oven roasted or steamed squash to blender and purée until creamy (add cooking water as needed to thin).

1. Follow the freezing and storing directions on page 75.

Perfectly Peachy

1 bag frozen organic peaches with skin

½ cup water

1. Steam peaches in water over medium heat until soft.
2. Add peaches to blender and purée until creamy (add cooking water as needed to thin).
3. Follow the freezing and storing directions on page 75.

Apple Purée

4 cups diced apples

1 cup water

1. Steam apples in water over medium heat until soft.
2. Add apples to blender and purée until creamy (add cooking water as needed to thin).
3. Follow the freezing and storing directions on page 75.

Pear Purée

4 cups diced pears

1 cup water

1. Steam pears in water over medium heat until soft.
2. Add pears to blender and purée until creamy (add cooking water as needed to thin).
3. Follow the freezing and storing directions on page 75.

Oven Roasted Pumpkin Purée

1 small baking pumpkin

1. Cut pumpkin in half
2. Roast flesh side down in oven on 350˚F for 30 minutes or until soft.
3. Remove flesh from outer shell and add to blender.
4. Add oven-roasted pumpkin and purée until creamy (add cooking water as needed to thin).
5. Follow the freezing and storing directions on page 75.

Kale Purée

2 bunches kale

½ cup water

1. Wash kale and remove stems.
2. Steam leaves with water for 7 minutes over medium-high heat.
3. Add kale to blender and purée until creamy (add cooking water as needed to thin).
4. Follow the freezing and storing directions on page 75.

Arugula Purée

4 cups fresh arugula

½ cup water

1. Steam arugula in water over medium heat until soft.
2. Add arugula to blender and purée until creamy (add cooking water as needed to thin).
3. Follow the freezing and storing directions on page 75.

Carrot Purée

(do not serve to an infant under the age of 3 months—see page 65)

4 cups diced carrots

1 cup water

1. Steam carrots in water over medium heat until soft.
2. Add to blender and purée until creamy (add cooking water as needed to thin).
3. Follow the freezing and storing directions on page 75.

Pastured Chicken Purée

1 whole pastured chicken

Any vegetables (onion, carrots, parsnips, celery)

1. In a large stock pot, add chicken and cut vegetables and cover with water.
2. Bring to a bowl, reduce heat, and cover.
3. Cook for 1–2 hours or until chicken is falling off the bone. Remove from heat.
4. Strain chicken, saving broth and vegetables (make a soup for later).
5. Remove chicken meat from bones. Add chicken meat to a blender.
6. Purée chicken, adding chicken broth until a thick and creamy consistency is reached.
7. Follow the freezing and storing directions on page 75.

Note: You will have the opportunity to thin the purée before serving, so keep it thick for freezing.

Beef Purée

1 lb pastured marbled chuck roast

½ cup water

1. Add chuck roast and water to slow cooker.
2. Cook on low heat for 8 hours or until the meat is falling apart.
3. Add all ingredients to a blender and blend until thick and creamy (add water or a home-made broth to thin as needed).
4. Follow the freezing and storing directions on page 75.

Note: You will have the opportunity to thin the purée before serving, so keep it thick for freezing.

Nourishing Bites for the Supported Sitter
(4–6 months)

This is a new and exciting time. Have fun and keep it simple. Remember that your baby is getting most of her nutrition from breast milk or formula. At this stage, you are introducing your child to a new dimension of life that will always be with her. Focus on the creating a safe and positive feeding environment without pressuring or forcing food.

- Thin purées with breast milk or formula as needed.
- Begin and end feedings with breast milk or formula.
- Allow the baby to show signs of hunger and fullness.
- Offer 1–2 tablespoons per meal, 1–2 meals per day.
- Introduce new foods every 4 days and then combine (optional).
- Add flavor (herbs, spice, texture, temperature changes) slowly.
- An infant might accept a strong flavor if it is mixed with familiar food (for example, an egg yolk with breast milk).
- Each recipe is enough for 1–2 meals and can be stored in the refrigerator for 1–2 days.

Fast Tips for Busy Moms

- Always have ready-to-mash produce on hand that does not need to be cooked (very ripe banana, avocado, and very ripe pear).
- Keep your freezer stocked with frozen organic produce (butternut squash, peas, carrots, broccoli, kale, peaches, strawberries, raspberries, blueberries, blackberries, mango, pineapple). Most of the preparation work has been done for you, saving you priceless time.
- If you do not want to soak and slow cook your beans, do not buy canned. You can find already cooked frozen beans in the freezer section.
- Freeze your own. If you use fresh, plan a prep day to cut, dice, soak, slow boil, and freeze for future use.
- Organize what you are making your family with the food item you are making for your baby. For example: steam carrots for your family but purée them for the baby.
- Instead of making apple purée, invest in an organic applesauce served in a glass jar.
- Instead of making pumpkin purée, invest in an organic pumpkin purée served in a glass jar.

Bone Broth
a staple for many recipes

4 lbs. pastured chicken (with bone and skin)

3 chopped onions

3 chopped carrots

4 chopped celery stalks

4 bay leaves

3 Tbsp. apple cider vinegar

12 cups filtered water

1. In a large stockpot, combine all ingredients and bring to a boil.
2. Reduce heat to medium-low and cover.
3. Cook for 1–2 hours or until meat falls off the bone.
4. Remove chicken from pot.
5. Let chicken cool, debone meat, replace skin and bones to broth.
6. Continue to cook broth on low for a couple hours covered.
7. Store chicken meat in a covered and labeled dish for 5 days. Use to make Chicken Pot Pie, Real Food Chicken Tenders, Asian Baby Burrito, Southwestern Baby Burrito, and many more recipes in this book.
8. Store broth up to 5 days and use in many recipes in this book.

Nutrition Tip: Bone broth is a staple in this book. It is a great source of vital minerals pulled from the bones of the chicken. The apple cider vinegar helps leach calcium, phosphorus, magnesium, and other nutrients into the broth, making them easy to digest.

Iron Rich Recipes

Baby's First Cereal

¼ cup gluten-free oat flour

¾ cup bone broth (page 81)

1 drop blackstrap molasses

1. In a saucepan, bring broth to a boil. Add oat flour and cook for 10 minutes, stirring constantly.
2. Let cool to a mild warm temperature.
3. Add breast milk or formula until you find a consistency that matches your child's developmental skills.
4. Add one drop of blackstrap molasses and mix.

Nutrition Tip: Blackstrap molasses is high in iron and other minerals. I use it to add additional iron to my children's food. However, one drop is enough to give your baby's food a healthy boost of iron. When shopping, look for organic, unsulfured blackstrap molasses. Two brands I enjoy are Grandma's Molasses or Brer Rabbit Molasses.

Sweet Pea

1 Tbsp. peas

1 Tbsp. mashed banana

1. Follow directions for preparing and serving bulk purées on page 75.
2. In a serving bowl, mix purées until well blended.
3. Add breast milk or formula until you find a consistency that matches your child's developmental skills.

Peas & Apples

1 Tbsp. peas

1 Tbsp. apple purée or applesauce

1. Follow directions for preparing and serving bulk purées on page 75.
2. In a serving bowl, mix purées until well blended.
3. Add breast milk or formula until you find a consistency that matches your child's developmental skills.

Pear & Chicken

1 Tbsp. pear purée

1 Tbsp. chicken purée

1 pastured egg yolk, cooked

¼ tsp. finely chopped basil

1. Follow directions for preparing and storing bulk purées on page 75.
2. In a serving bowl, mix purées until well blended.
3. Add breast milk or formula until you find a consistency that matches your child's developmental skills.
4. Mix in crumbled egg yolk.

Buttered Chicken

1 Tbsp. chicken purée

1 Tbsp. butternut squash

1 pinch finely chopped sage or thyme

1 drop blackstrap molasses

1. Follow directions for preparing and serving bulk purées on page 75.
2. In a serving bowl, mix purées, fresh herb, and molasses until well blended.
3. Add breast milk or formula until you find a consistency that matches your child's developmental skills.

Nutrition Note: Fresh herbs are full of vitamins, minerals and antioxidants. They help build strong bones and tough immune systems, and even aid in digestion. Hearty herbs such as rosemary and thyme make wonderful additions to meat and poultry dishes. Basil, mint, dill, parsley, and cilantro can add bursts of flavors to any fruit or vegetable recipe.

Baby's First Pot Pie

1 Tbsp. chicken purée

1 tsp. smashed sweet potato (from your dinner)

1 tsp. carrot purée

1 drop blackstrap molasses

1 pinch fresh herb (thyme or sage)

1. Follow directions for preparing and serving bulk purées on page 75.
2. In a serving bowl, mix purées, fresh herb and molasses until well blended.
3. Add breast milk or formula until you find a consistency that matches your child's developmental skills.

Chicken & Bananas

1 Tbsp. mashed banana

1 Tbsp. chicken purée

1 drop blackstrap molasses

1. Follow directions for preparing and serving bulk purées on page 75.
2. In a serving bowl, mix purées and molasses until well blended.
3. Add breast milk or formula until you find a consistency that matches your child's developmental skills.

Nutrition Tip: Adding a cube of chicken or beef purée will increase the absorption of the iron found in vegetables.

Chicken & Green Apples

1 Tbsp. applesauce

1 Tbsp. sweet pea purée

1 Tbsp. chicken purée

1 pastured egg yolk, cooked

1. Follow directions for preparing and serving bulk purées on page 75.
2. In a serving bowl, mix purées and yolk until well blended.
3. Add breast milk or formula until you find a consistency that matches your child's developmental skills.

Chicken with Roots

1 Tbsp. sweet potato (mashed from your dinner)

1 Tbsp. carrots

1 Tbsp. chicken purée

1 drop blackstrap molasses

1. Follow directions for preparing and serving bulk purées on page 75.
2. In a serving bowl, mix purées and molasses until well blended.
3. Add breast milk or formula until you find a consistency that matches your child's developmental skills.

Tangy Chicken

1 Tbsp. chicken purée

1 tsp. peach purée or ½ cup fresh or frozen peaches

1 pastured egg yolk, cooked

1. Follow directions for preparing and serving bulk purées on page 75.
2. If using frozen peaches, steam with water for 5 minutes and mash with a fork or blend in a blender.
3. In a serving bowl, mix purées until well blended.
4. Add breast milk or formula until you find a consistency that matches your child's developmental skills.

Iron Clad Beef

1 Tbsp. beef purée

1 Tbsp. apple purée or applesauce

1 pastured egg yolk, cooked

1 dash ground cumin

1. Follow directions for preparing and serving bulk purées on page 75.
2. In a serving bowl, mix purées, yolk, and cumin until well blended.
3. Add breast milk or formula until you find a consistency that matches your child's developmental skills.

Beefed up Iron

1 Tbsp. beef purée

1 Tbsp. pea purée

1 Tbsp. pear purée

1 drop blackstrap molasses

1. Follow directions for preparing and serving bulk purées on page 75.
2. In a serving bowl, mix purées and molasses until well blended.
3. Add breast milk or formula until you find a consistency that matches your child's developmental skills.

Beef with Vitamin C

1 Tbsp. peach purée

1 Tbsp. beef purée

1 pastured egg yolk, cooked

½ tsp. finely chopped rosemary or sage

1. Follow directions for preparing and serving bulk purées on page 75.
2. In a serving bowl, mix purées, fresh herb, and yolk until well blended.
3. Add breast milk or formula until you find a consistency that matches your child's developmental skills.

Baby's First Beef Stew

1 Tbsp. beef purée

1 Tbsp. carrots

1 Tbsp. peas

1 pinch finely chopped rosemary

1. Follow directions for preparing and serving bulk purées on page 75.
2. In a serving bowl, mix purées and rosemary until well blended.
3. Add breast milk or formula until you find a consistency that matches your child's developmental skills.

Bone Building Purées

Oats & Fruit

¼ cup gluten-free oat flour

¾ cup bone broth (see page 81)

1 Tbsp. banana purée

1 Tbsp. finely diced figs

1. In a saucepan, bring broth to a boil.
2. Add oat flour and figs.
3. Cook for 10 minutes, stirring constantly.
4. Add fruit purée and mix well.
5. Let cool to a mild but warm temperature.
6. Add breast milk or formula until you find a consistency that matches your child's developmental skills.

Other variations: substitute banana with 1 tablespoon of any fruit or vegetable purée.

Basil Whipped Banana

½ peeled banana

1 Tbsp. basil leaves

1. Add a ripe banana and basil to blender and whip until creamy.
2. Add breast milk or formula until you find a consistency that matches your child's developmental skills.

Cinnamon Sweet Potatoes

Baked Sweet Potato

1 sweet potato

¼ tsp. pastured butter

1 dash finely chopped cilantro

1. Bake potato in oven at 350°F for about 45 minutes, or until soft in the middle.
2. Remove flesh from skin.
3. Add butter and smash with a fork.
4. Add breast milk or formula until you find a consistency that matches your child's developmental skills.
5. Add cilantro and mix.

Cinnamon Smashed Sweet Potatoes

2 Tbsp. smashed sweet potato

1 dash cinnamon

1. Bake a sweet potato.
2. Remove flesh from peel and add cinnamon, mixing well.
3. Add breast milk or formula until you find a consistency that matches your child's developmental skills.

Creamy Butternut Squash

1 Tbsp. butternut squash

1 Tbsp. whole-fat yogurt

1. Follow directions for preparing and serving bulk purées on page 75.
2. In a serving bowl, mix purée and yogurt until well blended.
3. Add breast milk or formula until you find a consistency that matches your child's developmental skills.

Carrots & Bananas

¼ banana

1 Tbsp. carrot purée

1 Tbsp. whole-fat yogurt

1 dash finely chopped dill

1. Follow directions for preparing and serving bulk purées on page 75.
2. In a serving bowl, mix purée, banana, yogurt, and dill until well blended.
3. Add breast milk or formula until you find a consistency that matches your child's developmental skills.

Fall Harvest

1 Tbsp. baked sweet potato (from your baked potato)

1 Tbsp. pumpkin purée

1 dash finely chopped cilantro (optional)

1 pastured egg yolk, cooked

1. Follow directions for preparing and serving bulk purées on page 75.
2. In a serving bowl, mix purées, cilantro, and yolk until well blended.
3. Add breast milk or formula until you find a consistency that matches your child's developmental skills.

Pumpkin & Pear Purée

1 Tbsp. pumpkin purée

1 Tbsp. pear purée

1 pastured egg yolk

1 dash nutmeg or cinnamon (optional)

1. Follow directions for preparing and serving bulk purées on page 75.
2. In a serving bowl, mix purées, yolk, and spice until well blended.
3. Add breast milk or formula until you find a consistency that matches your child's developmental skills.

Pumpkins & Apples

1 Tbsp. pumpkin purée

1 Tbsp. applesauce or apple purée

1 pastured egg yolk

1 dash finely chopped rosemary

1. Follow directions for preparing and serving bulk purées on page 75.
2. In a serving bowl, mix purées, yolk, and rosemary until well blended.
3. Add breast milk or formula until you find a consistency that matches your child's developmental skills.

Orange Mania

1 Tbsp. peach purée or ½ cup fresh or frozen peaches

1 Tbsp. carrot purée or ½ cup fresh or frozen carrots

1 Tbsp. pumpkin purée

1 dash finely chopped mint or cilantro

1. Follow directions for preparing and serving bulk purées on page 75.
2. If using fresh or frozen ingredients, dice and steam in water for 5 minutes.
3. Blend all ingredients in blender, using cooking water to thin as needed.
4. Add breast milk or formula until you find a consistency that matches your child's developmental skills.

Brain Boosting Purées

Omega-3 Apples

½ apple or 1 Tbsp. apple purée

½ tsp. Atlantic mackerel, sardines (no salt added), or wild-caught salmon

½ tsp. pastured butter

1. Follow directions for preparing and serving bulk purées on page 75.
2. If using ½ apple, sauté apple in ¼ cup water and butter until soft and mash with a fork.
3. Mix pear and mackerel together until well blended.
4. Add breast milk or formula until you find a consistency that matches your child's developmental skills.

Fishing with Carrots

2 Tbsp. carrot purée

½ egg yolk, cooked

½ tsp. Atlantic mackerel, sardines (no salt added), or wild-caught salmon

1 dash finely ground ginger

1. Follow directions for preparing and serving bulk purées on page 75.
2. Mix carrot, egg yolk, fish, and ginger together until well blended.
3. Add breast milk or formula until you find a consistency that matches your child's developmental skills.

Green Pear

½ finely diced pear with skin

¼ cup water

½ ripe avocado, mashed

1. In a saucepan, cook pear in water for 3 minutes.
2. Remove pear from water and cool.
3. With a fork or in a blender, combine avocado until smooth.
4. Add breast milk or formula until you find a consistency that matches your child's developmental skills.

Brainy Pear

½ finely diced pear with skin

¼ cup water

½ tsp. butter

1 pastured egg yolk, cooked

1 dash finely ground ginger

1. In a saucepan, sauté pear in water and butter until soft. Mash with a fork.
2. Mix pear, egg yolk, and ginger together until well blended.
3. Add breast milk or formula until you find a consistency that matches your child's developmental skills.

Nutrition Tip: Pastured egg yolks are not only high in iron, but they are also a good source of Omega-3 fatty acids, making a great first food for your little one. Take comfort in knowing that you are providing a double dose of nutritional benefits every time you serve an egg yolk. Make sure the egg is pastured. See pages 62–64 to learn more about pastured animal products.

Creamed Fish

1 Tbsp. pear purée

¼ ripe avocado, mashed

½ tsp. Atlantic mackerel, sardines (no salt added), or wild-caught salmon

1. Follow directions for preparing and serving bulk purées on page 75.
2. Mix pear, avocado, and fish together until well blended.
3. Add breast milk or formula until you find a consistency that matches your child's developmental skills.

White Peaches with Sardines & Bananas

2 Tbsp. white peaches, finely diced

½ tsp. Atlantic mackerel, sardines (no salt added), or wild-caught salmon

¼ ripe banana, mashed

1 dash fresh cilantro, finely diced

1. Mix peaches, fish, banana, and cilantro together until well blended.
2. Add breast milk or formula until you find a consistency that matches your child's developmental skills.

Smashed Avocado

Smashed Avocado

½ ripe avocado, mashed with a fork

1. Add breast milk or formula until you find a consistency that matches your child's developmental skills,

Nutrition Tip: A ripe avocado should feel firm, not too mushy and with no air pockets. To cut, hold the avocado securely with one hand. Using a knife, cut in the center of the avocado lengthwise and around the seed. After you cut all the way around, hold the fruit with both hands and twist it open into two halves. To remove the seed, slip a spoon between the seed and flesh gently, removing the seed. If you are not going to use the entire fruit, leave the seed in and use the other half. The avocado will turn brown as it sits out, but you can simply slice off the brown before using.

Sweet & Chunky Avocado

½ ripe avocado, mashed with a fork

½ ripe banana

1. Mash and mix well for a new eater.
2. For more texture, dice the banana and gently mix into mashed avocado.
3. Add breast milk or formula until you find a consistency that matches your child's developmental skills.

Nutrition Tip: Adding a cooked pastured egg yolk to baby food recipes will increase healthy fat intake, Vitamin B, Vitamin K, Vitamin E, Vitamin A, Vitamin D, Iron, and Zinc. But don't waste the egg whites; look on page 174 to make a healthy Avocado Egg Salad for yourself.

Immunity Power Purées

Just Peaches

½ cup fresh or frozen organic peaches with skin, or 4 Tbsp. peach purée

1. If using purée, follow directions on page 75 for bulk purées.
2. Finely dice peaches, if using fresh or frozen.
3. Cook on low heat in a saucepan for 10 minutes or until warm and soft.
4. Add to blender and mix until smooth and creamy.
5. Add breast milk or formula until you find a consistency that matches your child's developmental skills.

Simply Butternut Squash

½ cup frozen organic butternut squash chunks, or 4 Tbsp. squash purée

1. If using purée, follow directions on page 75 for bulk purées.
2. Cook on low heat in a saucepan for 10 minutes or until soft.
3. Add to blender and mix until smooth, if using chunks.
4. Add breast milk or formula until you find a consistency that matches your child's developmental skills.

Simply Butternut

Just Peas & Carrots

1 Tbsp. pea purée

1 Tbsp. carrot purée

1. Follow directions for preparing and serving bulk purées on page 75.
2. In a serving bowl, mix purées until well blended.
3. Add breast milk or formula until you find a consistency that matches your child's developmental skills.

Skillet Smashed Pear

1 finely diced pear with skin

½ tsp. coconut oil

¼ cup water

1 drop blackstrap molasses (optional)

1. In a cast iron skillet, cook pear in coconut oil and water over medium heat until soft.
2. Add breast milk or formula until you find a consistency that matches your child's developmental skills.
3. Add one drop of blackstrap molasses and mix.

Nutrition Tip: Coconut oil is an excellent source of the medium fatty acid, lauric acid, and is one of the few food sources that contains it. Lauric acid is also found in human breast milk. When lauric acid enters the body it converts to monolaurin, a compound that kills harmful pathogens such as bacteria, viruses, and fungi.[2–4] Coconut oil is also great oil for cooking because it has a high smoke point (350°F). I also use it as a moisturizer for both my family and myself. Don't forget that we absorb nutrients through our skin as well.

Apples with Coconut

1 finely diced Gala apple

½ tsp. coconut oil

¼ cup coconut milk (filtered water works too)

1 dash cinnamon (optional)

1. In a cast iron skillet, cook apples with coconut oil, water, and cinnamon until soft.
2. Add breast milk or formula until you find a consistency that matches your child's developmental skills.

Nourishing Bites for the Unsupported Sitter
(7–9 months)

By now you should feel more comfortable and ready to expand. By 6 months of age, your baby's iron levels begin to decrease, requiring additional food sources of iron. These recipes are designed to increase the absorption of iron and other important minerals and vitamins for healthy growth.

Helpful Hints

- Thin purées with breast milk or formula as needed.
- Begin and end feedings with breast milk or formula.
- Allow the baby to show signs of hunger and fullness.
- The goal is to expose the infant to a large variety of foods and flavor.
- Offer a variety of food: 1–2 servings of vegetables, 1–2 servings of fruit, 1–2 servings of meat, and 1 serving of dairy.
- Introduce new foods every 4 days and then combine (optional).
- Add flavor.
- The guardian should not show a sign of food dislike.
- Each recipe is enough for 1–2 meals and can be stored in the refrigerator for 1–2 days.

Iron Rich Food

Scrambled Yolk and Cheddar

1 tsp. coconut oil

2 raw pastured egg yolks

1 Tbsp. shredded cheddar cheese

1. In a skillet over medium heat, melt coconut oil.
2. In a small mixing bowl, whisk together yolk and cheese.
3. Cook yolk mixture for 2 minutes on each side or until yolk is fully cooked.

Arugula Fried Eggs

1 tsp. pastured butter

1 whole pastured egg

1 pastured egg yolk

¼ cup pastured heavy cream, whole milk, formula, or breast milk

2 Tbsp. arugula purée

1. In a cast iron skillet, heat butter over medium heat.
2. In a bowl, mix eggs, cream, and arugula well.
3. Add arugula mixture to skillet and cook for 3 minutes on each side.
4. Serve warm.

Nutrition Tip: Throw in an extra egg yolk to any recipe that has eggs. The extra yolk will provide your baby with an extra nutrient-dense punch to build powerful brains and strong muscles.

Baby's First
Chicken Salad

Baby's First Chicken Salad

1 Tbsp. finely shredded and chopped pastured chicken (cooked but chilled)

2 tsp. whole-fat pastured yogurt

¼ tsp. finely diced dill

1. In a serving bowl, mix all ingredients together and serve immediately.

Chicken with Arugula & Pear

1 Tbsp. pear purée

½ Tbsp. arugula purée

1 Tbsp. chicken purée

1. Follow directions for preparing and serving bulk purées on page 75.
2. In a serving bowl, mix purées until well blended.
3. Add breast milk or formula until you find a consistency that matches your child's developmental skills.

Parsley & Bananas

1 tsp. parsley, finely chopped or puréed

½ diced banana

1 pastured egg yolk

1. Follow directions for preparing and serving purées on page 75.
2. In a serving dish, mix banana, parsley, and yolk until well blended.
3. Add breast milk or formula until you find a consistency that matches your child's developmental skills.

Dilled Peas

¼ tsp coconut oil

1 Tbsp. fresh or frozen peas (coarsely chopped or as-is)

1 pinch freshly chopped dill

1. In a cast iron skillet, heat coconut oil over medium heat.
2. Add peas and cook for 5 minutes, constantly stirring.
3. Toss with dill before serving.
4. Serve warm with shredded and diced chicken, pork, or beef.

Pumpkin & Raspberry with Chicken

2 Tbsp. pumpkin purée

4 fresh or frozen raspberries

1 Tbsp. chicken purée

1 drop blackstrap molasses (optional)

1 pinch finely chopped parsley

1. In a saucepan, cook purées and raspberries until 165°F is reached, constantly stirring.
2. Add one drop of blackstrap molasses and herbs, mixing well.

Note: Try not to mash the raspberries up too much. Use them as your texture component by keeping them chunky.

Peas & Apples with Basil

¼ cup fresh or frozen peas

1 Tbsp. apple purée or applesauce

1 drop blackstrap molasses

1 dash finely chopped basil

1. In a saucepan, heat peas and apples over medium heat, constantly stirring and slightly mashing peas for 5 minutes.
2. Remove from heat.
3. Add molasses and basil and mix until well blended.

Nutrition Tip: Vitamins and minerals are found in the edible peels of fruits and vegetables. I recommend using edible peels (apple, pear, plum, peach) when making your baby foods, but chop them very finely. Skins can be a potential choking hazard if left too big.

Minced Pork & Apples

1 Tbsp. applesauce

1 tsp. minced pastured pork (use a fatty cut of meat)

1 dash cinnamon

1. In a bowl, mix all ingredients until well blended.
2. Serve warm.

Nutrition Tip: When feeding an infant meat, choose juicy meats such as the dark meat of chicken. Any meat served to an infant should be shredded and then finely diced to prevent choking. An infant can use her fingers to rake the meat and self-feed. To make it softer, mix the meat with applesauce or banana. Not only will this help with self-feeding, but the vitamin C in the fruit will increase the absorption of iron in the meat.

Curried Chicken & Apricots

½ cup diced unsulfured apricots

2 Tbsp. water

1 Tbsp. chicken purée (or diced chicken from your dinner)

¼ tsp. curry powder

1 dash cumin

1. Dice apricots and steam in water for 10 minutes, covered.
2. Follow directions for preparing and serving bulk purées on page 75.
3. Add chicken purée or diced chicken to apricots until an internal temperature of 165°F is reached.
4. Add apricots, chicken, curry, and cumin to blender. Blend until thick and creamy.
5. Add breast milk or formula until you find a consistency that matches your child's developmental skills.

Cheesy Chicken & Rosemary

2 Tbsp. butternut squash

1 Tbsp. ricotta cheese

½ tsp. finely chopped rosemary

1 tsp. chopped chicken (cooked to 165°F from your meal)

1. Follow directions for preparing and serving bulk purées on page 75.
2. In a serving bowl, mix purée, ricotta cheese, rosemary, and chicken until well blended.
3. Add breast milk or formula until you find a consistency that matches your child's developmental skills.

Nutrition Tip: Compare the sodium (salt) content of both ricotta and cottage cheeses while shopping. I have found that organic Ricotta cheese tends to be lower in sodium per serving, but this does vary from brand to brand. Always select the lower amount of sodium per serving. Also, consider the texture between ricotta and cottage cheeses and what your baby prefers. Ricotta is smooth, while cottage cheese varies in texture.

Bone Building

First Avocado Dip

½ avocado

1 Tbsp. whole-fat yogurt

1. Blend ingredients together in a blender.
2. Add breast milk or formula until you find a consistency that matches your child's developmental skills.

Apple & Oats Pudding

½ cup uncooked oatmeal

1 cup pastured whole milk (or water or bone broth)

1 Tbsp. whole-fat yogurt

1 Tbsp. applesauce

¼ tsp. cinnamon

1. In a saucepan over medium heat, cook oats and milk for 7 minutes or until soft and smooth, mixing frequently.
2. Mix yogurt, apple, and cinnamon into oatmeal.

First
Avocado Dip

Blueberry Mousse

Real Strawberry Yogurt

4 large strawberries (without stems)

¼ cup whole-fat yogurt

1. Crush strawberries with a fork or blend in a blender.
2. Swirl crushed strawberry into yogurt.

Figs & Berries

½ cup diced strawberries (without stems)

1 diced fig

1 tsp. fresh herb (cilantro, mint, or basil)

¼ cup water

1. In a saucepan, sauté figs and strawberries with water for 2 minutes.
2. Blend mixture with fresh herbs in blender until smooth.

Blueberry Mousse

1 cup fresh or frozen blueberries

¼ cup heavy pastured cream

¼ tsp. cinnamon

1. Add ingredients to blender and mix on high until thick and creamy.
2. Serve immediately.

Berry Almonds

½ cup almonds

1½ cups frozen raspberries

½ cup heavy pastured cream

1. Soak almonds overnight, rinse, and drain.
2. Add almonds to a blender and mix on high until they turn to a creamy paste.
3. Mix in raspberries and cream until well blended.
4. Serve immediately.

Strawberry & Almond Purée

8 raw almonds

4 large strawberries

1 tsp. fresh herbs (basil, cilantro, or mint)

1. Pulse almonds in a blender until finely chopped.
2. Add strawberries and herbs and mix until you find a consistency that matches your child's developmental skills.

Strawberry and
Almond Purée

Green Apples & Cheese

1 Tbsp. applesauce

1 Tbsp. kale purée

1 Tbsp. organic Ricotta cheese or cottage cheese

1. Follow directions for serving and preparing purées on page 75.
2. Mix purées with cheese until well blended.
3. Add breast milk or formula until a consistency matches your child's developmental skills.

Broccoli & Banana Purée

½ cup broccoli florets

½ very ripe banana

1. In a saucepan, add water and broccoli florets.
2. Steam broccoli florets for 5 minutes, covered.
3. Remove broccoli for remaining water and pulse (finely chop) broccoli and banana in a blender until texture matches your child's developmental skills.

Chopped Minted Watermelon & Kale

¼ cup diced watermelon

1 tsp. finely chopped fresh or frozen kale

1 tsp. chopped mint

1. In a serving bowl, mix all ingredients together.

Calcium Spiked Squash

1 Tbsp. butternut squash purée

1 Tbsp. kale purée

1 pinch chia seed meal

1 pinch cilantro

1. Follow directions for preparing and serving bulk purées on page 75.
2. In a serving bowl, mix purées, cilantro, and chia seed meal until well blended.
3. Add breast milk or formula until you find a consistency that matches your child's developmental skills.

Nutrition Tip: Chia seeds are high in omega-3 fatty acids and calcium. It is important to buy the meal (ground chia seeds) over the whole seed for easier digestion and nutrient absorption. Even better—soak the whole seeds for a couple hours to increase digestion and absorption.

Smooth Kale & Bananas

½ banana, mashed

1 Tbsp. kale purée

1 Tbsp. whole-fat yogurt

1. Follow directions for preparing and serving bulk purées on page 75.
2. In a serving bowl, mix banana, kale, and yogurt until well blended.
3. Add breast milk or formula until you find a consistency that matches your child's developmental skills.

Brain Boosting

Brainy Oats

½ cup uncooked oatmeal

1 cup whole-fat milk (or broth or water)

¼ very ripe banana

1 egg yolk, cooked

1. In a saucepan over medium heat, cook oats and milk for 7 minutes or until soft and smooth, mixing frequently.
2. Mash banana and mix into oatmeal.
3. Serve warm topped with crumbled egg yolk.

Nutrition Tip: Are you wondering what to do with the egg whites yet? I use the egg yolks because they are nutrient dense. For many years, feeding egg whites to an infant was frowned upon, due to potential allergens. The current recommendations claim it is ok to introduce any allergens to a low-risk infant before year one. You can add some chopped egg white to your recipes. However, if you still feel uncomfortable, check out the Avocado Egg Salad for you on page 174.

Smashed Berries, Chia, & Apples

1 Tbsp. applesauce or apple purée

5 frozen or fresh raspberries (any berry will do)

1 pinch chia seed meal

1. Mix ingredients together until well blended, slightly smashing berries to a consistency perfect for your little one.

Buttered Wild Salmon

2 Tbsp. butternut squash purée

1 tsp. wild salmon

½ tsp. finely chopped rosemary leaves

¼ tsp. fresh lemon juice

1. Follow directions for preparing and serving bulk purées on page 75.
2. Add all ingredients to a blender and mix until well blended.
3. Add breast milk or formula until you find a consistency that matches your child's developmental skills.

Go Green Go Fish

1 Tbsp. kale purée

2 Tbsp. apple purée or applesauce

1 tsp. no-salt sardines

1. Add all ingredients to a saucepan and cook for 7 minutes over medium heat, stirring frequently.

Immunity Power

Sautéed Bananas with Coconut & Pumpkin Spice

½ tsp. virgin unrefined coconut oil

½ banana, diced

1 dash pumpkin spice or to taste

1. Heat coconut oil in skillet over medium-low heat.
2. Sauté banana until slightly golden.
3. Sprinkle with pumpkin spice to taste.

Skillet Fried Ginger Pear & Apple Purée

1 Tbsp. coconut oil

1 diced Gala apple

1 diced Bosc pear

¼ cup coconut milk

1. In a cast iron skillet, heat coconut oil over medium heat.
2. Add pears and apples and cook for 5 minutes or until warm and soft.
3. Add fruit mixture and coconut milk to blender and mix well.
4. Serve with shredded and chopped juicy pork or chicken.

Sautéed Bananas

Tangy Carrot and
Pineapple Purée

Tangy Carrot & Pineapple Purée

2 Tbsp. carrot purée

¼ cup finely diced pineapple

1. Follow directions for preparing and serving bulk purées on page 75.
2. Mix carrot and pineapple together until well blended.

Nutrition Tip: Every baby is different. Some babies might prefer thin purées, while others go right for the chunky foods. The type of texture served should be determined by the feeding skills of your child. If your child is ready, slowly increase the texture by coarsely chopping and puréeing less. Go slow and enjoy watching your child discover new sensations.

Cranberry Applesauce

½ cup diced fresh cranberries

2 finely diced Gala apples with peels

1 cup coconut water

¼ tsp. cinnamon

1. Combine all ingredients in a saucepan.
2. Cook covered over medium heat until cranberries and apples are soft.
3. Uncover and cook for 5–10 minutes.
4. Add more coconut water to reach a consistency for your little one.

Strawberry-Pomegranate Purée

½ cup fresh or frozen strawberries (without stems)

¼ cup fresh pomegranate seeds

¼ tsp. fresh lemon juice

1 pinch fresh mint

1. Add all ingredients to blender and mix until smooth.

Whipped Bananas & Blueberries

½ very ripe banana

1 Tbsp. finely chopped blueberries

1. Chill banana in refrigerator for 2 hours.
2. Remove banana peel.
3. Add to blender on high until creamy.
4. Top whipped bananas with chopped blueberries.

Tropical Punch Purée

¼ cup diced apple

¼ cup diced pineapple

¼ cup fresh or frozen raspberries

1. Pulse all ingredients in a blender to a consistency perfect for your little one.

Grapes with Arugula Swirl

1 Tbsp. Arugula purée

1 cup seedless red grapes

1. Follow directions for preparing and serving bulk purées on page 75.
2. Add grapes to blender and purée.
3. Put grape purée in serving bowl and swirl in arugula.

Butternut Squash with Cilantro & Coconut

2 Tbsp. butternut squash purée

½ tsp. finely chopped cilantro

½ tsp. coconut

1. Follow directions for preparing and serving bulk purées on page 75.
2. In a mixing bowl or blender, mix all ingredients until well blended.

Stewed Apricots

16 dried unsulfured apricots

¼ cup water

¼ tsp. vanilla extract

1 tsp. coconut oil

1. Finely dice apricots.
2. In a bowl, mix water and vanilla extract together.
3. In a saucepan, heat coconut oil over medium heat.
4. Add apricots and water to mixture.
5. Cover and cook over medium heat for 7 minutes or until soft.
6. Serve warm.

Fuji Apples & Apricots with Rosemary

½ cup diced Fuji apples

10 dried unsulfured apricots

½ tsp. fresh-squeezed lemon juice

1 Tbsp. pastured butter

¼ tsp. diced rosemary leaves

1. Coarsely dice apples (with skins) and apricots.
2. Add all ingredients to sauce pan over medium heat.
3. Cover and cook for 7 minutes, stirring frequently.

Peach & Raspberry Lemon Lush

2 Tbsp. finely diced fresh or frozen peaches

1 Tbsp. finely diced fresh or frozen raspberries

¼ tsp. fresh lemon juice

1. Mix all ingredients together and serve chilled.

Nourishing Bites for the Crawler
(10-12 months)

At this stage, most babies are ready for thicker foods, which they can "rake" with their hands or pick up with their fingers. The recipes in this section are designed to encourage self-feeding and maximize nutrition.

Feeding Tips

- Allow the baby to show signs of hunger and fullness.
- Daily intake of food will vary from meal to meal and day to day.
- Don't forget to offer a snack.
- Continue to introduce new foods every 4 days and then combine.
- Continue to expose the child to a variety of textures and tastes.
- Continue to breastfeed based on your baby's needs.

Iron Rich Meals

Egg Soaked French Toast

½ banana, mashed

2 pastured egg yolks

¼ cup breast milk, formula, or pastured cream (if using gluten-free bread, you may need to use more liquid)

1 dash cinnamon

1 slice sourdough bread (gluten-free bread can substitute)

2 Tbsp. coconut oil

1. Mix banana, egg, milk, and cinnamon until well blended.
2. Place bread in a shallow bowl and pour mixture over bread.
3. Let the bread soak up the egg mixture for 10 minutes or until the bread is soggy.
4. Heat coconut oil in cast iron skillet over medium heat.
5. Using a large spatula, transfer soaked bread into skillet (otherwise, it will fall apart).
6. Cook the bread on each side for 7 minutes or until golden brown.
7. Remove from skillet and cool.
8. Cut into strips.
9. Serve with Strawberry-Pomegranate Purée (page 126).

Pumpkin Crusted Chicken Pot Pie

2 Tbsp. flour

2 cups whole-fat milk, divided

2 cups bone broth (or chicken broth)

1 cup diced carrots

2 tsp. salt, divided

2 cup diced fully cooked chicken

1 tsp. poultry seasoning

Edna Inspired Crust

1 cup self-rising flour

¼ cup pastured butter

¼ cup pumpkin purée

1 tsp. baking powder

1. Whisk flour with 1 cup milk until well blended.
2. In a saucepan over medium heat, add milk mixture and broth, mixing until well blended.
3. Add carrots, 1 teaspoon salt, and poultry seasoning. Bring to a low boil and cook for 10 minutes, stirring occasionally.
4. Add chicken, remove from heat, and transfer to casserole dish.
5. In a mixing bowl, combine melted butter, remaining milk, flour, pumpkin purée, baking powder and 1 teaspoon of salt (or to taste), and mix well. Evenly add this mixture to the casserole dish, but do not mix.
6. Cook on 350°F for 45 minutes. Brown under broiler until golden brown. Serve over mashed potatoes.

Chicken Pot Pie

First Shepherds Pie

2 Tbsp. pastured butter

1 cup diced onion

½ diced bell pepper (red, yellow, green, or combination)

1 cup diced carrots

1 lb. pastured ground beef

1 cup beef bone broth

3 Tbsp. tomato paste

1 Tbsp. chili powder

1 tsp. cumin

1 cup frozen or fresh corn kernels

3 cups mashed potatoes

½ cup heavy cream (whole-fat milk works too)

1 tsp. pastured butter

1 pastured egg

1. In a medium size cast iron skillet, heat butter over medium heat.
2. Add onions and peppers and cook until onions are translucent. Add carrots and cook for 5 minutes. Add beef and cook for 5 minutes, breaking it up with a wooden spoon.
3. Stir in broth, tomato paste, chili, and cumin, cooking for 5 minutes. Stop and taste—add salt and pepper as needed. Spread out evenly in pan.
4. In a mixing bowl, mix potatoes with cream, butter, and egg. Stop and taste—add salt and pepper to potatoes. Spoon potatoes over meat mixture.
5. Broil skillet for 10 minutes or until potatoes are golden.

Baby's First Meatballs

1 lb. ground beef

2 pastured eggs

½ cup Parmesan cheese

½ cup diced sweet onions

2 cloves garlic

⅓ cup bread crumbs

1. In a large mixing bowl, combine all ingredients, mixing well.
2. Roll meat mixture into ½-inch balls.
3. Sauté in olive oil for 10 minute or until cooked thoroughly (165°F), gently stirring.
4. Drain on a plate with a paper towel.

To Freeze for Later:

1. Transfer meatballs to a cookie sheet, cover with wax paper and freeze for 2 hours.
2. When frozen, remove from cookie sheet and store in freezer-safe contain labeled with date and name.

Meatball and Kale
Soup

Meatball & Kale Soup

8 cups chicken bone broth (see page 81)

3 coined or diced carrots

6 oz Delallo Gluten-Free Orzo (or favorite orzo)

¼ cup Parmesan cheese

1 cup frozen chopped kale

½ batch of Baby's First Meatballs, cooked (see page 135)

salt to taste

1. In a large stockpot, boil carrots and pasta in broth until pasta is done.
2. Refer to the directions on the pasta box for cooking duration, as all pasta cooks at different rates.
3. Slowly stir in Parmesan cheese.
4. Add fully cooked meatballs and chopped kale.
5. Salt to taste.

Bone Building

Broccoli & Cheddar Quiche

6 pastured eggs

2 pastured egg yolks

1 cup cheddar cheese, divided

½ cup heavy pastured cream

1 serving Thyme, Broccoli, & Cheddar Skillet without the cheese (page 140)

1. In a large bowl, mix eggs and additional egg yolks with cream and ¾ cup cheese.
2. Add Thyme, Broccoli, & Cheddar Skillet mixture to eggs, mixing well.
3. Divide mixture into prepared (greased or lined) muffin tins (makes about 12 mini quiches).
4. Cook on 350°F for 30 minutes in muffin tins, or until quiche is golden brown.

Cauliflower Gratin

1 cup chopped cauliflower

¼ cup panko bread crumbs

2 Tbsp. pastured butter, melted and divided

1 cup grated Gruyere cheese, divided

¼ cup heavy cream (whole milk works well too)

1. In a bowl, mix all ingredients (minus 1 tablespoon butter and 1 cup cheese) until well blended.
2. Melt remaining tablespoon butter in cast iron skillet over medium heat.
3. Add all ingredients to cast iron skillet and cover.
4. Cook for 20 minutes at 350°F, stirring occasionally.
5. Remove lid, add remaining cheese, and broil until golden brown.

Tex Mex

¼ avocado

1 Tbsp. plain whole-fat yogurt

1 pastured egg yolk

¼ cup mashed pinto beans

1 Tbsp. shredded cheddar cheese

1 dash cumin

1. In a bowl, mix all ingredients together until well blended.
2. Serve chilled.
3. Top with Simple Salsa, optional (page 158).

Thyme, Broccoli, & Cheddar Skillet

1 cup finely chopped broccoli florets

¼ cup finely diced sweet onion

1 Tbsp. pastured butter

1 tsp. thyme

¼ cup shredded cheddar cheese

1. Chop (or pulse) onion and broccoli to a consistency that is perfect for your little one.
2. Heat butter in cast iron skillet over medium heat. Add broccoli, onion, and thyme.
3. Sauté for 5 minutes.
4. Remove from heat. Add cheddar cheese and cover to melt. Serve warm.

Broccoli and Cheddar Skillet

Refried Beans with Melted Cheddar

2 cups dry pinto beans

8 cups bone broth

1 diced sweet onion

1 cup crushed tomatoes

2–3 minced garlic cloves

1 Tbsp. cumin

1 Tbsp. pastured butter

½ cup cheddar cheese

1. Rinse beans and soak in water overnight. Drain water and rinse beans after soaking.
2. Add beans, broth, onions, tomatoes, garlic, and cumin. Cook over medium-low heat for 2½ hours, or until beans are soft. Drain bean mixture, saving broth for later use.
3. In a cast iron skillet, heat butter over medium heat.
4. Add bean mixture with 1 cup of bean broth.
5. Cook beans, stirring and mashing until you reach a consistency your baby prefers. Add broth as needed.
6. Top with cheese and place under oven broiler for 3 minutes or until cheese is melted.

Nutrition Tip: Soaking legumes (all beans) overnight will reduce the phytate. Phytate is naturally found in many grains and inhibits the absorption of minerals. Soaking eliminates the phytate in the beans.

Oven Roasted Sweet Potato with Apples & Thyme

2 Tbsp. pastured butter

1 Tbsp. coconut oil

1 cup diced sweet potato

1 ½ cups diced granny smith apple

2 Tbsp. water

1 Tbsp. fresh thyme

1. Melt butter with coconut oil and mix together.
2. In a bowl, mix all ingredients together and transfer to a casserole dish.
3. Cover and bake 350°F for 15 minutes, or until soft.

Creamy Kale & Apple Dip

1 cube apple purée or 1 Tbsp. applesauce

1 cube kale purée

3 Tbsp. whole-fat yogurt

1. Follow directions for defrosting and serving bulk purées.
2. In a bowl mix purées and yogurt until well blended.
3. Serve chilled with favorite fruit or thinly cut sticks of veggies.

Mung Bean and
Cheddar Wedges

Mung Bean & Cheddar Wedges

1 cup Moong Dal (split mung beans without husk, lentils can substitute)

2 cups bone broth

1 Tbsp. pastured butter

1 cup finely diced onion

½ tsp. cumin

¼ tsp. turmeric

2 pastured eggs

½ cup pastured heavy cream (whole-fat milk can substitute)

½ cup cornmeal

1½ cup shredded extra sharp cheddar cheese, divided

1. Soak beans overnight, rinse and drain. Combine beans and bone broth to saucepan. Bring to boil, reduce heat, cover and simmer for 20 minutes.
2. Drain beans and set aside.
3. Heat butter in a medium size cast iron skillet.
4. Add onion to skillet and fry until translucent.
5. Mix cumin and turmeric into beans.
6. In a large mixing bowl, combine all ingredients (only 1 cup cheese).
7. Grease a pie pan. Pour mixture into pie pan and press down on mixture. Sprinkle the remaining cheese over mixture.
8. Bake for 30 minutes at 350°F. Allow to cool and then cut into wedges. Serve warm or cold.

Sweet Potato Sticks

1 sweet potato

1 Tbsp. pastured butter

choice of seasonings (garlic powder, cumin, paprika, cinnamon)

1. Cut potatoes into ½-inch thick fingers or sticks.
2. Melt butter and coat potato fingers with it.
3. On a cookie sheet, bake potato sticks for 30 minutes on 350°F or until potatoes are soft.
4. Bake an additional 10 minutes for crunchy sticks.

Fried Sweet Potato & Pumpkin Cakes

2 cups shredded sweet potato

1 Tbsp. pastured butter

¼ cup finely chopped onion

1 garlic clove, minced

1 tsp. thyme

2 pastured eggs

½ cup pumpkin purée

4 Tbsp. flour

salt to taste

1 Tbsp. coconut oil

1. Peel and shred sweet potato.
2. Heat butter in skillet and sauté onion for 3 minutes.
3. Add garlic and thyme and cook for 1 minute (careful not to burn garlic).
4. In a bowl, combine eggs, pumpkin, flour, and salt.
5. Make patties out of ¼ cup mixture.
6. Heat coconut oil in a skillet over medium heat.
7. Fry for 4–6 minutes on each side, until golden brown.
8. Drain on a paper towel. Serves 2 adults and 1–2 children.

Clementine Sweet Potatoes & Cilantro

1 cup sweet potatoes, coarsely diced

¼ cup fresh clementine juice (orange juice works too)

1 Tbsp. pastured butter

1 Tbsp. chopped cilantro

1. In a saucepan, stew potatoes in juice and butter over medium heat until soft and liquid evaporates.
2. Remove from heat and stir in cilantro.
3. Serve warm.

Sweet Potato & Kale Cups

½ cup raw kale leaves, finely chopped

1 tsp. olive oil

1 dash salt (kelp works well too)

1 cup finely diced sweet potato

1 medium-ripe banana

1 Tbsp. pastured butter, melted

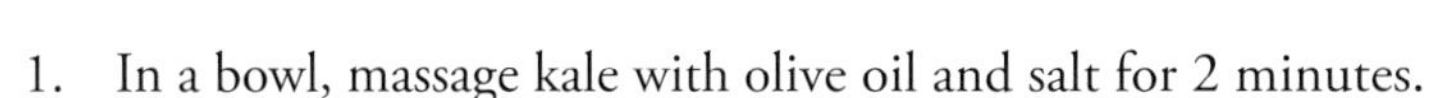

1. In a bowl, massage kale with olive oil and salt for 2 minutes.
2. Add remaining ingredients to bowl and mix well.
3. Transfer veggies to greased or paper-lined muffin tins.
4. Bake at 350°F for 45 minutes or until potatoes are tender.

Brain Boosting

Avocado Dip

½ avocado

½ tsp. cilantro

1 pastured egg yolk, boiled

1 dash cumin

1. Add all ingredients to a blender and mix until well blended.
2. Serve chilled or at room temperature.

Banana Cakes

½ cup Pumpkin Buckwheat Pancake batter (page 165)

¼ tsp. chia seeds

½ banana (not too ripe or it will fall apart during cooking)

1 tsp. coconut oil

1. Prepare ½ cup of pancake batter and add chia seeds to mixture.
2. Slice banana into ¼-inch slices and dip both sides into batter.
3. In a cast iron skillet, heat coconut oil over medium heat.
4. Add bananas and sauté for 3 minutes on each side or until golden brown.

Brain Powered Grilled Cheese

3 pastured egg yolks, beaten

1 tsp. dried seaweed, crumbled (optional)

¼ cup heavy pastured cream (substitute whole milk)

1 slice of bread (gluten-free bread can substitute)

1 Tbsp. unsalted pastured butter

1 Tbsp. squash purée

⅓ cup pastured shredded cheese

1. Beat egg yolks, seaweed, and cream until well blended.
2. Cut bread in half and soak for 5–10 minutes in egg mixture until soggy.
3. Melt butter in skillet over medium heat.
4. Using a spatula, transfer soaked bread to skillet.
5. Cook on both sides for 7 minutes, until yolk is cooked and bread is browned.
6. Follow directions for defrosting purées.
7. Spread purée on the inside of the sandwich and add cheese.
8. Close the sandwich with the other ½ slice of bread.
9. Cover and cook until cheese is melted.
10. Remove from heat and cut into thin strips.
11. Serve immediately.

Soaked Nut & Banana Berrywich

¼ banana

4 raspberries

1 Tbsp. any nut or seed butter (sunflower, pumpkin, peanut, almond, etc.)

¼ tsp. chia seeds

1 slice sourdough bread (gluten-free bread can substitute)

¼ cup breast milk, formula, goat milk, or cow milk

1. Mix banana, raspberries, chia seeds, and sunflower butter until smooth.
2. Place bread in a shallow serving bowl and spread mixture on bread.
3. Pour milk over bread and let it soak until moist.
4. Serve immediately.

Pan-Fried Trout

12 oz. trout, cut into fillets

salt and pepper to taste

1 Tbsp. pastured butter

juice of 1 lemon

1. Season fish with salt and pepper. In a cast iron skillet, heat butter over medium heat.
2. Working in batches, add fish to skillet, cooking on each side for 3 minutes until golden brown. Drizzle fish with lemon juice.
3. Serves 2 adults and 1–2 children.

Mema's Cornbread Dressing Cakes

2 Tbsp. pastured butter, divided

½ cup diced celery

½ cup diced onion

1 cup gluten-free cornbread mix (Bob's Red Meal)

¼ cup chia or flaxseed meal

1 tsp. poultry seasoning

1 cup whole-fat pastured milk

1½ cups cubed, cooked chicken

3 pastured eggs, lightly beaten

1. In a cast iron skillet, melt 1 tablespoon butter over medium heat.
2. Cook onion and celery for 10 minutes, until onions are translucent.
3. Remove vegetable mixture and set aside.
4. Melt remaining butter in same skillet.
5. In a large mixing bowl, combine all remaining ingredients, including vegetable mixture.
6. Pour batter into hot skillet.
7. Bake for 30 minutes at 350°F or until golden brown.
8. Serves 2 adults and 1–2 children.

Mema's Cornbread
Dressing Cakes

Bright Eyes Carrot Bake

¼ cup bone broth

2 cups grated carrots

½ cup diced onion

½ cup diced celery

½ tsp. rosemary

1 tsp. thyme

1 cup gluten-free cornbread mix (Bob's Red Meal)

¼ cup chia seed or flaxseed meal

3 pastured eggs

1 tsp. salt or to taste

1. In a saucepan, add bone broth, carrots, onions, and celery.
2. Cook until onions are soft.
3. Add herbs and mix well.
4. Remove from heat.
5. Mix in cornmeal, chia or flaxseed meal, and eggs and mix well. Salt to taste.
6. Spread mixture into greased glass baking dish.
7. Bake for 20 minutes at 350°F or until golden brown.
8. Serves 2 adults and 1–2 children.

Immunity Power

Cucumber & Mint Salad

½ cup coarsely diced cucumbers

¼ cup whole-fat pastured yogurt

1 Tbsp. chopped mint

1 tsp. ground walnuts (optional)

1. In a bowl, mix all ingredients.
2. Serve chilled.

Gingered Pear Fingers

1 tsp. coconut

¼ tsp. fresh grated ginger

1 pinch cinnamon

½ pear, cut into strips

1. In an oven-safe skillet over medium heat, melt coconut oil with ginger and cinnamon for 1 minute.
2. Remove from heat.
3. Add pears to skillet and coat with coconut, ginger, and cinnamon.
4. Broil pears in skillet for 10 minutes.
5. Serve warm.

Lemon & Raisin Coated Pear Fingers

1 tsp. pastured butter

¼ cup raisins

½ tsp. fresh lemon juice

½ pear, cut into strips

1. In an oven-safe skillet over medium heat, melt butter with raisins and lemon for 1 minute.
2. Remove from heat.
3. Add pears to skillet and coat with coconut, raisins, and lemon.
4. Broil pears in skillet for 10 minutes.
5. Serve warm.

Basil, Avocado, & Tomato Salad

½ cup cherry tomatoes, cut into thin slivers

1 diced avocado

1 Tbsp. finely diced red onion

1 Tbsp. finely chopped basil

¼ tsp. balsamic vinegar

1. In a bowl, mix all ingredients together.
2. Serve chilled.

Pear Fingers

Simple Salsa

½ cup finely diced tomatoes

1 tsp. finely diced scallions (green section only)

1 tsp. finely diced green peppers or chilies

1 Tbsp. finely diced cilantro

salt to taste

1. In a bowl, mix all ingredients together and serve with dipping vegetables or tortillas.
2. Use for Tex-Mex Meatloaf topping (page 191).

Nutrition Tip: Remember that variety is not necessarily feeding your infant different foods each day. It is also offering the same foods, cooked or cut differently. Children like what is familiar to them, and it is your job to make it familiar. Don't give up if your child refuses food.

Mango & Red Pepper Salsa

2 cloves garlic, minced

2 Tbsp. rice vinegar

juice of ½ fresh lime

1 cup diced sweet red pepper

2 cups frozen diced mango

¼ cup diced scallion

¼ cup chopped cilantro

1. Combine garlic, vinegar, and lime.
2. In another bowl, mix remaining ingredients well. Toss dressing into mango and pepper mixture.
3. Serve salsa with your favorite chips, over a cooked white fish (page 187), or Grilled Shrimp Tacos (page 188).

Oven Roasted Cauliflower & Mint Salad

½ cup oven roasted diced cauliflower, room temperature (page 162)

1 Tbsp. finely chopped mint

½ tsp. minced garlic

¼ tsp. rice vinegar

1. In a bowl, mix all ingredients and serve at room temperature or chilled.

Curried Apples & Cauliflower

1 tsp. pastured butter

1 diced Gala apple

1 cup diced cauliflower

¼ tsp. curry powder

1. Heat butter in a cast iron skillet over medium heat.
2. Sauté apples and cauliflower with curry for 7 minutes, or until tender.
3. Serve warm.
4. Serve with shredded chicken or pork.

Pear and Ginger Slaw

Pear & Ginger Slaw

2 red pears

¼ tsp. fresh ginger root, shredded

¼ tsp. cinnamon

¼ cup coconut milk

1. Add all ingredients to a blender.
2. Pulse on low to create a chunky, chopped texture.
3. Serve chilled.

Tropical Salad

1 diced kiwi

2 diced strawberries

¼ tsp. shredded coconut

¼ tsp. cilantro

1. In a bowl, mix all ingredients until well blended. Serve chilled.

Simple Vegetable Oven Roasting Chart

Oven Roast 350°F	Asparagus	Broccoli	Brussels Sprouts	Cauliflower
Cut	Snap woody ends off	Chop crowns (1–2-inch sections)	Trim the tips and cut in half	Chop crowns (1–2-inch sections)
Flavor	Olive oil with salt and pepper	Olive oil with salt and pepper	Olive oil with salt and pepper	Olive oil with salt and pepper
Time Cook on Baking Sheets	10–15 minutes, shaking pan every 5–10 minutes to rotate asparagus	20–30 minutes depending on size, shaking pan every 5–10 minutes to rotate broccoli	20–30 minutes depending on size, shaking pan every 5–10 minutes to rotate sprouts	20–30 minutes depending on size, shaking pan every 5–10 minutes to rotate cauliflower

Sweet Potatoes	Red Pepper	Summer Squash	Winter Squash
Cut into chunks or wedges	Whole	Slice into long flat strips	Cut into chunks or wedges
Honey and Maple syrup	N/A	Olive oil with salt and pepper	Honey and Maple syrup
30–45 minutes depending on size, shak-ing pan every 5–10 minutes to rotate potatoes	30 minutes, turning until all sides are black. Cool completely and peel off skin.	15–20 minutes depending on thickness, flipping once	30–45 minutes depending on size, shaking pan every 5–10 minutes to rotate squash

*Use the Herb and Spice Guide on page 16 and 100 Ways to Serve Ten Fruits/Vegetables on page 8 to create your own recipes.

Nourishing Bites for the Walker

(>12 months)

- Most recipes feed 2 adults and 1–2 children.
- Allow the baby to show signs of hunger and fullness.
- An infant's appetite will vary from meal to meal and day to day.
- Using purées of the past is a great way to introduce a variety of familiar foods (for example–use a favorite purée as a pasta sauce).
- Introduce new foods every 4 days and then combine.
- Continue to add flavor, texture and variety.
- Continue to use recipes from the earlier age categories.

from the mom tip

"I like to put a plate of veggies, fruit, and nuts on an easily accessible table at snack time. My daughter can still get a healthy snack even while going non-stop."

—Betty Jo, mommy to Kennedy, age 1, North Carolina

Scrumptious Day Starters

Pumpkin Buckwheat Pancakes

1 cup buckwheat flour

1 cup coconut milk (whole-fat milk will work too)

1 pastured egg, slightly beaten

¼ cup pumpkin purée

1 tsp. baking powder

½ tsp. salt

1 tsp. cinnamon

¼ tsp. ginger

1 tsp. vanilla extract

1 Tbsp. coconut oil

1. In a bowl, mix all ingredients except coconut oil together.
2. Heat coconut oil in griddle over medium-high heat.
3. Pour ⅓ cup batter for each pancake onto the hot griddle.
4. Cook 1–2 minutes on each side, turning when edges bubble.
5. Serve with yogurt for dipping or Strawberry-Pomegranate Purée (page 126)

Strawberry & Mascarpone Bruschetta

1 cup chopped strawberries

1½ tsp. balsamic vinegar

2 tsp. chopped fresh mint

¾ cup mascarpone cheese

1 Tbsp. local honey

salt to taste

1. In a mixing bowl, toss strawberries, vinegar, and mint together and set aside.
2. In another bowl, combine cheese, honey, and salt.
3. Spread cheese mixture on whole grain toast, mini bagels, or your favorite morning bread.
4. Top with strawberry vinegar mixture.

Pear & Fig Oat Cup

1 chopped pear

½ cup oatmeal

2 pastured eggs, slightly beaten

½ cup whole-fat yogurt

1 tsp. vanilla extract

1 tsp. cinnamon

½ cup finely diced figs, dates, or raisins

1. In a bowl, mix all ingredients well.
2. Divide mixture among 6 large greased or lined muffin tins.
3. Bake for 35 minutes on 350°F until browned.

Pear and Fig
Oat Cups

Arugula & Goat Cheese Muffins

½ cup finely chopped arugula

1 pastured egg and 1 pastured egg yolk, beaten

¼ cup gluten-free corn bread meal (no sugar added)

1.5 oz. goat cheese

2 tsp. pastured butter

¼ cup thinly sliced cherry tomatoes

salt and pepper to taste

1. In a bowl, mix all ingredients together well.
2. Divide among 6 small greased or lined muffin cups and bake at 350°F for 15–20 minutes until browned.

Ya-Ya's Roasted Potato Frittata

1 large russet potato with peel

1 Tbsp. olive oil

salt, pepper, and cayenne pepper to taste

1 Tbsp. butter

½ cup diced onion

½ cup diced green peppers

¼ cup diced mushrooms

4 pastured eggs

½ cup cheddar cheese

1. Cut potato into ½-inch slices, coat with olive oil, and add your salt, pepper, and cayenne pepper. Roast in oven at 450°F for 15 minutes. Set aside.
2. In a cast iron skillet, heat butter over medium heat.
3. Add onion and green pepper, sautéing for 3–5 minutes until soft.
4. Add mushrooms and cook for 10 minutes.
5. In a mixing bowl, whisk eggs and cheese.
6. Pour egg mixture over vegetables in the skillet, scraping egg mixture from side to middle of skillet until egg mixture is cooked.
7. Place potato slices on top of frittata.
8. Broil in oven until egg is golden brown.

Raspberry, Yogurt, & Banana Pop

2 bananas

1 cup whole-fat plain yogurt

1 cup fresh or frozen raspberries

2 strawberries to garnish

1. Blend bananas, yogurt, and raspberries in blender until thick and creamy.
2. Pour into paper cups or frozen pop molds (makes 3 large or 6 small paper cups).
3. Slice strawberries and slide down the sides of mold or cup.
4. Freeze with wooden craft stick for 4 hours.

Nutrition Tip: Changing the types of foods you serve at different meals will also offer variety to your child. A frozen breakfast on a stick is a fun way to get nutrients into your child's belly. Don't be afraid to serve breakfast for dinner or lunch to change up the routine.

Almond Raspberry Mousse Pop

1 cup almonds

3 cups frozen raspberries

1 cup heavy pastured cream

1. Soak almonds overnight, rinse, and drain.
2. Blend almonds until they turn into a creamy paste.
3. Mix in raspberries and cream, and blend until well blended.
4. Pour into paper cups or frozen pop molds (makes 3 large or 6 small paper cups).
5. Freeze with wooden craft stick for 4 hours.

Salads: Make Your Taste Buds Dance

Summer Squash Ribbon Salad

2 squash (or 1 yellow squash and 1 green zucchini)

¼ cup red wine vinegar

½ tsp. peanut oil (avocado and olive oil both work well too)

2 tsp. spicy mustard

¼ cup finely diced parsley

½ tsp. salt (optional)

1 ripe avocado, diced

¼ cup feta cheese

¼ cup pumpkin seeds (or your favorite seeds)

1. Using a vegetable peeler, peel squash, making long ribbons.
2. In a bowl, mix vinegar, oil, mustard, parsley, and salt well.
3. Add squash and avocado, gently tossing with dressing.
4. Top with feta cheese and pumpkin seeds.

Toddler's Chicken
Salad

Toddler's Chicken Salad

2 cups diced chicken breast, fully cooked

1 cup chopped sweet red peppers (or chopped sweet apples)

1 cup chopped cucumber

1 cup whole-fat plain yogurt

1½ tsp. spicy brown mustard

½ cup raisins

¼ cup diced red onion

¼ cup diced fresh dill

1 tsp. salt or to taste

pepper to taste

1. In a bowl, mix all ingredients together well.

Nutrition Tip: When serving a green leafy salad to a toddler, let her assemble the salad. Offer the ingredients on separate plates and let her decide what she will eat. Yes, I know it is extra work, but it is totally worth it. You will also be surprised at her creations; and better yet, she will eat her creations. Typically children do not like their ingredients mixed together, but they may eat it if they assemble it themselves.

Chopped Arugula, Basil, & Avocado Salad

1 cup finely chopped basil

1 cup finely chopped arugula

½ cup diced fresh mozzarella

½ cup cherry tomatoes (halved)

1 diced avocado

salt and pepper to taste

1. In a bowl, mix all ingredients together.

Avocado Egg Salad

4 hard boiled eggs, peeled and halved

1 Tbsp. rice vinegar

1 tsp. spicy mustard

½ tsp. salt (optional)

1 avocado, halved

¼ cup chopped scallions

1. Remove egg yolks and use in other baby food recipes. Dice egg whites.
2. In a medium mixing bowl, combine vinegar, mustard, salt, and half of the avocado. Mix until smooth.
3. Dice remaining avocado.
4. Add diced egg, diced avocado, and scallions to the bowl and mix gently.
5. Serve on a bed of lettuce or with your favorite crackers.

Avocado Egg Salad

Figs & Feta Salad

½ cup olive oil

¼ cup balsamic vinegar

2 Tbsp. local honey

3 cups favorite salad mix (I like field greens with arugula)

¼ cup diced scallions

½ cup dried unsulfured figs, diced

½ cup plain feta cheese, crumbled, or to taste

1 ripe avocado

1. In a small mixing bowl, combine oil, vinegar, and honey, whisking until well blended.
2. In a large salad bowl, toss scallions and salad mix with dressing.
3. Top with figs and feta cheese.

Nutrition Tip: See page 173 for tips on how to serve salad to toddlers.

Southwest Kale & Black Bean Salad

1 bunch kale

juice of 1 lime

1 tsp. salt

1 cup black beans (soaked and slow boiled or frozen)

⅔ cup fresh or frozen corn kernels

1 cup fresh cilantro

2 cups diced tomatoes

1 cup diced scallions

1 diced jalapeño pepper (optional)

¼ cup peanut oil

1 Tbsp. cumin

1 diced avocado

1. De-stem kale leaves and finely chop.
2. Message kale leaves in lime juice and salt for 2 minutes.
3. Combine all ingredients in a large mixing bowl (except avocado) and refrigerate for 4–6 hours.
4. Before serving, toss and taste.
5. Add salt to taste, if needed.
6. Add diced avocado and toss.

Fresh Bean Salad

1 medium red onion, thinly sliced

1 medium cucumber, diced

2 medium tomatoes, diced

¼ cup chopped cilantro

1 cup white beans (soaked overnight and slow boiled or frozen)

1 chopped avocado

juice of 2 limes

salt and pepper to taste

1. Combine onions, cucumbers, tomatoes, and cilantro in a medium-sized bowl.
2. Mix in beans, avocado, and lime juice.
3. Add salt and pepper to taste.
4. Serve chilled.

Mid-Day Energy Boosters

Spiced Almond Slivers

2 cups slivered raw almonds

1 tsp chili powder

¼ tsp. cinnamon

1 dash cayenne pepper (optional)

salt to taste

1 Tbsp. pastured butter

1. In a bowl, combine all ingredients and spread out onto a baking sheet.
2. Cook at 350°F for 2 hours, stirring every 30 minutes until almonds are browned.

Slow-Boiled Pinto Beans

2 cups dry pinto beans

1 Tbsp. pastured butter

1 cup diced onion

1 cup diced celery

2 cups diced tomatoes

4½ cups bone broth page 81 (water will work too)

2 slices uncured bacon

1 Tbsp. cumin

1. Soak beans in water overnight, rinse, and drain.
2. In a large stockpot, add butter, onions, and celery over medium heat.
3. Cook until onions are translucent, for about 5 minutes.
4. Add tomatoes and cook for 3 minutes.
5. Add broth, beans, bacon, and cumin.
6. Increase to medium-high heat and bring to boil.
7. Reduce heat to low, cover, and cook for 2 hours or until beans are soft.
8. Serve over mashed potatoes.

Real Food Chicken Tenders

½ cup flour

¼ cup chia seed meal

1 cup Panko bread crumbs (salt and pepper to taste)

3 large pastured eggs, beaten

½ cup whole-fat pastured milk

1 lb. boneless chicken thighs, cut into 1 × 3-inch pieces.

2 Tbsp. coconut oil

2 Tbsp. pastured butter

1. Mix flour, chia seed meal, and panko bread crumbs in a shallow bowl. Salt and pepper to taste.
2. In another shallow bowl, mix egg and milk until well blended.
3. Working in batches, coat chicken with flour mixture, then dip each piece in the egg mixture, coating both sides. Finally, coat both sides again with flour mixture.
4. Heat coconut oil and butter in a 12-inch cast iron skillet over medium-high heat.
5. Add chicken to pan and cook for 5 minutes on each side until fully cooked and golden brown.
6. Drain chicken on a plate with a paper towel.

Nutrition Tip: Cooking food in a cast iron skillet increases the iron content of the food. This is a simple way to increase iron in your diet.

Southwestern Burrito Baby

1 cup shredded chicken or pork

⅓ cup corn

¼ cup Slow-Boiled Pinto Beans (page 180), or black beans

½ tsp. cumin

½ tsp. chili powder

dash of salt (optional)

2 Tbsp. chopped bell peppers

2 Tbsp. diced scallions

1 cup grated cheese (your favorite)

wonton wrappers

3 tsp. coconut oil

1. In a bowl, mix together all ingredients except wonton wrappers and coconut oil.
2. Place wanton wrapper in a diamond shape and add ¼ cup of filling horizontally in center of wrap.
3. Fold bottom corner over filling. Fold in side corners.
4. Brush top corner with water and roll up wrap tightly. Seal roll with top flaps.
5. In a skillet, heat oil over medium heat.
6. Working in batches, add rolls to skillet.
7. Cook for 5 minutes on each side or until golden brown.
8. Drain on paper towels.

Fish Nuggets

12 oz. wild-caught white fish (tilapia, etc.)

1 tsp. Cajun seasoning (optional)

1 cup Panko bread crumbs

¼ cup chia or flaxseed meal

salt and pepper to taste

2 large pastured eggs

¼ cup pastured butter

¼ cup coconut oil

1. Cut fish into 1-inch cubes, toss with Cajun seasoning, and set aside.
2. Mix bread crumbs and chia seed meal together in a shallow bowl.
3. Add salt and pepper to taste.
4. Beat eggs in another shallow bowl.
5. Dredge fish in bread crumbs, evenly coating both sides. Dip in egg, and then coat again with bread crumbs.
6. In a cast iron skillet, heat coconut oil and butter on medium-high heat.
7. Add fish and fry for 3 minutes on each side, until golden brown and fully cooked.

Toddler's Favorite Pasta Sauce

½ cup cooked pasta of choice (gluten-free pasta works too)

4 Tbsp. baby's favorite purée (for the sauce)

1. Cook pasta according to package directions.
2. Drain pasta and set aside.
3. Follow directions for defrosting purées on page 75.
4. Heat purée in saucepan over medium heat until hot.
5. Add pasta and mix well.
6. Serve warm.

Nutrition Tip: Change up your pasta each time you make a pasta dish! This is a simple way to add variety. There are so many fun shapes and sizes of pasta—have fun.

Toddler's Favorite Quinoa

2 Tbsp. baby's favorite purée

¼ cup cooked quinoa (from your dinner)

1. Follow directions for defrosting purées on page 75.
2. In a saucepan over medium heat, mix quinoa with purée.
3. Serve warm with shredded and diced chicken, beef, or pork.

Pumpkin, Carrot, & Quinoa

1 Tbsp. pumpkin purée

1 Tbsp. carrot purée

1 Tbsp. cooked quinoa (substitute any grain from your dinner)

1 dash pumpkin spice

1. Follow directions for defrosting bulk purées on page 75.
2. In a serving dish, mix quinoa with purée. Serve warm with shredded or diced chicken, beef, or pork.

EZ Mac & Cheese

1 (12-oz.) box elbow macaroni (gluten-free pasta works too)

2 Tbsp. flour or cornstarch

1 cup shredded sharp white cheddar cheese

½ cup mascarpone cheese (or cream cheese)

1 tsp. spicy mustard

1 Tbsp. pastured butter

2 cups whole-fat pastured milk

1 tsp. salt, or to taste

1. In a large pot, boil pasta until almost done (al dente), drain, and set aside.
2. Mix flour with shredded cheese, mascarpone cheese, and mustard until flour is well blended into cheeses. Set aside.
3. In a saucepan, melt butter over medium heat and add milk.
4. Add cheese mixture to milk, constantly stirring for 8–10 minutes or until creamy. If you want a thinner sauce, add more milk. If you want a thicker sauce, use less milk. Add salt to taste. Add pasta to sauce and mix well.

Very Gouda Mac & Cheese

1 (12-oz.) pkg. elbow pasta (gluten-free pasta works too)

4 slices thick, uncured, pastured bacon

2 cups shredded Gouda cheese

2 cups shredded Gruyère cheese

2 Tbsp. flour, divided

3 cups whole-fat pastured milk

salt to taste

1. In a large stockpot, cook pasta until almost done (al dente).
2. In a large cast iron skillet, add bacon and cook over medium low heat until crispy on both sides.
3. Remove bacon from pan, leaving bacon drippings, and drain on a paper towel. After bacon cools, crumble and set aside.
4. In a large mixing bowl, combine Gouda cheese, 1 cup of Gruyère cheese, and 1 tablespoon flour until well blended.
5. Over low heat, whisk remaining 1 tablespoon flour into bacon grease until well blended and bubbly.
6. Gradually add milk and cheese mixture, whisking constantly until the sauce is melted. Sauce should not be thick.
7. Add salt and pepper to taste. Remove from heat and fold in pasta.
8. Sprinkle top with remaining 1 cup Gruyère cheese and thin bacon bits.
9. Bake uncovered at 350°F for 20 minutes.

Dinnertime Favorites

Herbed Avocado Pasta Sauce

2 avocados, diced

1 cup packed basil

½ cup packed cilantro

1 tsp. lemon juice

1–2 cloves garlic

10 almonds

2 Tbsp. mild olive oil

salt to taste

1. In a blender, mix all ingredients until smooth and creamy.
2. Use as a sauce for your favorite cooked pasta.
3. Serve immediately.

White Fish Topped with Mango & Red Pepper Salsa

12 oz. favorite wild white fish

2 Tbsp. coconut oil

Mango & Red Pepper Salsa (page 158)

1. Completely wrap fish and coconut oil in parchment paper.
2. Transfer fish packet onto baking sheet.
3. Cook at 350°F for 10 minutes or until fish is fully cooked.
4. While fish is cooking, prepare Mango & Pepper Salsa.
5. Before serving, top with salsa.

Salmon Sayz

12 oz. (total) wild-caught salmon fillets

1 Tbsp. coconut oil

1 cup diced pineapples

1 cup diced tomatoes

1. Wrap salmon fillets, pineapple, tomatoes, and coconut oil in parchment paper.
2. Place salmon packet on baking sheet.
3. Cook for 15 minutes at 375°F or until fully cooked.

Grilled Shrimp Tacos

5 bamboo skewers

1 lb. fresh or frozen shrimp (16–20 shrimp)

1 Tbsp. pastured butter, melted

6 6-inch tortillas

Mango & Red Pepper Salsa (page 158)

1 avocado, sliced

1. Soak bamboo skewers in water for approximately 1 hour.
2. Put shrimp on skewers and grill over medium heat until completely cooked (2 minutes on each side).
3. Melt butter and brush onto shrimp while cooking.
4. Assemble tacos with tortillas, salsa, and fresh avocado slices.

Lemon Chicken with Asparagus

2 Tbsp. pastured butter

¼ cup coconut oil

½ cup flour (or cornstarch)

salt and pepper to taste

4 chicken thighs, boneless

1 cup bone broth

4 garlic cloves, minced

1 bunch asparagus, cut into 1-inch sections

¼ cup fresh parsley

juice of 1 lemon

1. In a cast iron skillet, heat butter and coconut oil over medium-high heat.
2. Put flour in a shallow bowl and season with salt and pepper to taste.
3. Dredge both sides of chicken thighs in flour. Add chicken thighs to pan and cook for 3 minutes on both sides, or until golden brown. Remove and let drain on a plate with a paper towel. Reduce heat to low.
4. Add 1 tablespoon of remaining flour from dredging to oil in skillet, scraping the sides and bottom. Stir in flour for 3 minutes, or until dissolved.
5. Add broth, garlic, and asparagus and mix until well blended.
6. Place chicken back in pan, cover, and cook for 1 more minute. Remove from heat and let stand for 10 minutes, covered.
7. Mix in parsley and lemon juice.

Spicy (optional) Peanut Chicken Skillet

1 Tbsp. pastured butter

1 cup finely chopped onion

1 cup finely chopped celery

4 cloves garlic, minced

1 Tbsp. ginger, minced

½ cup chicken bone broth

6 chicken thighs with skin and bone (about 1.5 lbs.)

3 Tbsp. natural peanut butter (no sugar or salt added)

½ cup coconut milk

2 Tbsp. fresh lime juice

2 Tbsp. low-sodium soy sauce

1 diced jalapeño pepper (optional)

1 tsp. curry powder

1 cup finely chopped red bell pepper

1 cup snow peas

½ cup fresh chopped cilantro leaves

½ cup fresh chopped basil

1 cup chopped peanuts

1. In a cast iron skillet, heat butter over medium heat.
2. Add onions and celery, cooking for 5 minutes.
3. Add garlic and ginger, cooking for 1 minute.
4. Add bone broth and bring to a boil.
5. Add chicken and remove from heat.
6. In a bowl combine peanut butter, coconut milk, lime juice, soy sauce, jalapeño pepper, and curry and mix well.
7. Pour over chicken, cover, and cook in oven at 350°F for 30 minutes (occasionally stirring).
8. Add bell pepper and snow peas and cook, covered, for 10 minutes.
9. Brown under broiler for 5 minutes.
10. Stir in fresh herbs and peanuts before serving.

Tex-Mex Meatloaf

1 lb. pastured ground beef, bison, or venison

½ cup chopped onion

½ cup chopped bell peppers (red, yellow, green, or combination)

½ cup diced tomatoes

1 jalapeño pepper, diced (optional)

3 Tbsp. homemade taco seasoning or 1 packet taco seasoning (any variety)

½ cup cornmeal

½ cup heavy pastured cream (or whole milk)

2 pastured eggs, beaten

¼ cup fresh chopped cilantro

1 cup favorite salsa (Simple Salsa, page 158)

½ cup Asadero cheese (or Monterey Jack)

1. Preheat oven 400°F.
2. In a large mixing bowl, combine meat, onion, peppers, tomatoes, jalapeño pepper, seasoning, cornmeal, cream, egg, and cilantro. Mix until well blended.
3. Form a 2-inch thick rectangular shaped meatloaf in a baking dish without touching the sides of dish.
4. Bake for 30 minutes at 350°F, remove, and top with salsa and cheese.
5. Return to oven for another 10 minutes or until it reaches an internal temperature of 165°F.
6. Serve with Avocado Dip (page 149).

Umphress Stew

2 Tbsp. pastured butter

½ medium sweet onion, diced

1 lb. pastured ground beef

1 cup diced carrots

1 cup green beans

1 cup okra

8 cups crushed tomatoes

1–2 cups cooked pasta (your choice of amount and type—we like elbow noodles or spiral pasta)

salt and pepper to taste

Note: The best part about Umphress stew is that you can add any vegetables you have on hand. My mother has made this with corn and potatoes.

1. In a large stockpot, sauté onions in butter on medium heat for about 5 minutes, or until onions are translucent.
2. Add beef and brown in onion and butter mixture, breaking up meat with a wooden spoon, but leaving large chunks.
3. Add remaining vegetables and tomatoes and cook for 15 minutes, or until vegetables are soft.
4. Add pasta, salt, and pepper (traditionally this recipe has a lot of pepper).

Beef, Kale, & Chickpea Curry

1 Tbsp. coconut oil

1 cup finely chopped onions

4 cloves garlic, minced

1 tsp. curry powder

1 Tbsp. minced ginger

1 lb. pastured stewing beef, cut into ½-inch cubes

2 cups cooked chickpeas

1 cup beef broth

1 bunch kale

1. In a skillet, heat oil and cook onions for 3–5 minutes, until soft.
2. Mix in garlic, curry powder, and ginger. Cook for 1 minute.
3. Add beef, chickpeas, broth, and onion mixture to slow cooker.
4. Cook on low for 8 hours, or on high for 4 hours, until beef is tender.
5. Taste and add salt to your liking.
6. De-stem kale leaves and boil for 3 minutes.
7. Rinse kale with cold water. Wring, chop, and store covered in the refrigerator until needed.
8. Add kale, cover, and cook on high for 20 minutes.

Southern Roots Chop Suey

4 Tbsp. peanut oil (or coconut oil)

1 medium sweet onion, diced

3 celery stalks, diced

1 small cabbage, thinly sliced

2 cups fresh mung bean sprouts

1 lb. pork butt, cut into 1-inch thick strips

1 cup bone broth (page 81)

2 Tbsp. low-sodium soy sauce

1 Tbsp. low-sodium Teriyaki sauce

1. In a skillet or wok, heat 2 tablespoons of the peanut oil.
2. Add onion and celery, cooking for 3–5 minutes or until translucent.
3. Add cabbage and bean sprouts, cooking another 5 minutes, stirring occasionally.
4. Remove vegetables and set aside.
5. Reheat skillet over medium heat with remaining peanut oil.
6. Add pork and cook for 5 minutes on each side, or until brown.
7. Add broth, soy sauce, and Teriyaki sauce.
8. Cover and cook for 5 minutes.
9. Add cooked vegetables and gently stir.

Pork & Greens

2 bunches greens (collard, mustard, kale, or combination)

4 country-style pork ribs

½ cup bone broth or water

salt and pepper to taste

1. Remove leaves from stems.
2. Rinse well, removing dirt from inner part of leaves.
3. In a large stockpot, combine all ingredients.
4. Cover and simmer on medium-low heat for 2 hours.
5. Continually check water level, adding more if necessary. The greens should not be saturated with water; there should be just enough on the bottom for the pork and greens to cook in their own sauce.
6. Salt and pepper to taste.
7. Remove from heat when the pork is falling off the bones.

Toddler-Style Beverages

Food is fun. Drinks are fun too! In my home, it was always water or milk. Boring, I know. I felt like a broken record, and needed to give more options in the beverage department in my own home. I had to come up with a better solution. Not only are these fun, but they are great for children who are slow to transition to different tastes and textures.

Real Food Flavored Milk

What child does not want flavored milk? The problem with flavored milk is that it is usually high in added sugar and comes with a side of artificial colorings. Here's my solution—Real Food Flavored Milk using real fruit cubes! For every 4-ounce serving of milk, add 3 fruit cubes. If you are done making purées and freezing cubes, never fear. Just fill ice cube trays with diced fresh berries, cover with milk, and freeze for at least 4 hours.

Strawberry Cubes

2 cups frozen strawberries

1. Blend strawberries in blender until liquid.
2. Divide into silicon ice cube trays and freeze for 4 hours.
3. Remove cubes from tray. Label a freezer-safe container with date and contents.
4. Store in freezer for up to 6 months.

Blackberry Cubes

2 cups frozen blackberries

1. Blend blackberries in blender until liquid.
2. Divide into silicon ice cube trays and freeze for 4 hours.
3. Remove cubes from tray. Label a freezer-safe container with date and contents.
4. Store in freezer for up to 6 months.

Raspberry Cubes

2 cups frozen raspberries

1. Blend raspberries in blender until liquid.
2. Divide into silicon ice cube trays and freeze for 4 hours.
3. Remove cubes from tray.
4. Label a freezer-safe container with date and contents.
5. Store in freezer for up to 6 months.

Peach Cubes

2 cups frozen peaches

1. Blend peaches in blender until liquid.
2. Divide into silicon ice cube trays and freeze for 4 hours.
3. Remove cubes from tray.
4. Label a freezer-safe container with date and contents.
5. Store in freezer for up to 6 months.

Genuine Strawberry Milk

3 strawberry cubes

½ cup whole-fat pastured milk (milk substitutes work well too!)

ice

1. Combine all ingredients.
2. Let sit at room temperature for 20 minutes. Stir and serve.

Peaches & Milk

3 peach cubes

½ cup whole-fat pastured milk (milk substitutes work well too!)

ice

1. Combine all ingredients.
2. Let sit at room temperature for 20 minutes. Stir and serve.

Berry Blaster

1 cube strawberry

1 cube blackberry

1 cube raspberry

½ cup whole-fat pastured milk (milk substitutes work well too!)

ice

1. Combine all ingredients.
2. Let sit at room temperature for 20 minutes. Stir and serve.

Real Food-Flavored Water

I love adding fruit and veggie cubes to water. Get the child involved and let them pick the color of their cube or cubes. Children enjoy watching the cube slowly melt into their water. Infusing flavor into water is a great way to make small changes for a child that is extremely sensitive to taste variation.

Watermelon Cubes

2 cups watermelon

1. Blend watermelon in blender until liquid.
2. Divide into silicon ice cube trays and freeze for 4 hours.
3. Remove cubes from tray. Label a freezer-safe container with date and contents.
4. Store in freezer for up to 6 months.

Kiwi Cubes

2 cups kiwi

1. Blend kiwi in blender until liquid.
2. Divide into silicon ice cube trays and freeze for 4 hours.
3. Remove cubes from tray. Label a freezer-safe container with date and contents.
4. Store in freezer for up to 6 months.

Carrot Cubes

1 cup carrot juice (freshly juiced or store bought)

1. Divide into silicon ice cube trays and freeze for 4 hours.
2. Remove cubes from tray. Label a freezer-safe container with date and contents.
3. Store in freezer for up to 6 months.

Melon Balls

3 watermelon cubes

½ cup water

ice

1. Combine all ingredients.
2. Let sit for 20 minutes. Stir and serve.

Kiwi Melon

2 watermelon cubes

1 kiwi cube

½ cup water

ice

1. Combine all ingredients.
2. Let sit for 20 minutes. Stir and serve.

Bunny Hop

3 carrot cubes

½ cup water

ice

1. Combine all ingredients.
2. Let sit for 20 minutes. Stir and serve.

Lemon Raspberry Water

3 raspberry cubes

2 lemon slices

½ cup water

ice

1. Combine all ingredients.
2. Let sit for 20 minutes. Stir and serve.

Melon & Mint Crush

1 cup diced melon

1 tsp. chopped mint

1. Freeze diced melon for about 1 hour.
2. Combine melon and mint in a bowl and crush.

Honey Lemonade Slushy

1 lemon, juiced

1 tsp. honey (or to taste)

1 cup water

½ cup ice cubes

1. Blend all ingredients in a blender.
2. Serve over ice with a slice of lemon.

Strawberry Lemonade Slushy

1 serving Honey Lemonade Slushy (previous page)

2 strawberry cubes (page 196)

1. Add strawberry cubes to Lemonade Slushy.

Clementine & Mint

2 clementines, peeled

1 tsp. finely chopped mint

1 cup water

½ cup ice

1. Crush clementine in the bottom of a glass, mixing in mint.
2. Add water to clementine mixture.
3. Divide ice among 2 kid-size cups.
4. Pour clementine mixture into cups with ice.

Cucumber & Mint

½ cup cucumber thinly sliced

1 tsp. finely chopped mint

1. Divide ingredients among 2 kid-size cups.
2. Add ice and fill with water.

Nutrient-Dense Treats

Who doesn't like dessert? Seriously, I am not going to tell you to avoid sugar. As long as we consider moderate intake at special occasions, it is ok. If I told you to avoid sugar, it would set the stage for forbidding foods to your child. In fact, I encouraged my children to try treats when offered to them. If they bring candy home from school events, we put it in a special place in the kitchen, giving them access to it around the clock. Believe it or not, they don't crave it, because we never gave the candy power. However, dessert does not always have to be sugar. Here are a couple recipes that are nutrient dense and are great little treats.

Frozen Chocolate & Peanut Butter Banana Bites

1 ripe banana

½ cup natural peanut butter, melted (peanuts should be the only ingredient)

½ cup semi-sweet chocolate chips, melted

1. Cut banana into ½-inch think coins.
2. Drizzle melted peanut butter and chocolate over the bananas.
3. Freeze for 2 hours on a cookie sheet.

Banana & Coconut Ice Cream

4 frozen bananas (without peels)

½ cup unsweetened coconut milk

1 tsp. vanilla extract

1. In a blender, mix bananas, milk and vanilla until smooth.
2. Top with Perfectly Peachy (page 76) or Figs & Berries (page 115).

Traditional Custard

3 cups pastured whole-fat milk

3 pastured whole eggs

3 pastured egg yolks

¾ cup local maple syrup

1 tsp. vanilla extract

1. In a heavy saucepan, heat milk to a soft boil, stirring occasionally.
2. In a blender, mix eggs, egg yolks, and maple syrup until creamy.
3. Slowly add egg mixture to warm milk, stirring after each small addition.
4. Add vanilla and set aside.
5. Pour custard mixture into 8 custard cups.
6. Place the cups in a large baking pan and pour very hot water into the pan, about halfway up the sides of the cups.
7. Bake for 50 minutes, or until custards are set.

Sweet Almond Kisses

1 cup raw almonds

1 Tbsp. chia seeds

¼ cup coconut flour or oatmeal flour

1 Tbsp. local honey

1 tsp vanilla

1. Grind almonds and seeds in a blender until ground into a flour.
2. Add coconut flour, honey, and vanilla.
3. Pulse until blended.
4. Form into bite-size kisses and chill for 30 minutes, covered.

Frozen Pineapple on a Stick

1 whole pineapple

wooden craft sticks

1. Remove outer layer of pineapple.
2. Cut pineapple into 3–4 × 1-inch slices.
3. Slide pineapple onto craft stick.
4. Arrange in a single layer on a cookie sheet covered with wax paper.
5. Freeze for 4 hours, covered.
6. Store in a freezer-safe container, properly labeled with name and date.

Nutrition Tip: Frozen Pineapple on a Stick and frozen celery sticks are great teething treats. Not only are they safe, but they offer a sense of taste while teething.

Fig Bread Pudding

2 croissants, torn into 1 inch pieces (from your favorite local bakery or homemade)

2 pastured eggs and 1 pastured egg yolk, beaten

½ cup pastured cream

1 tsp. cinnamon

1 tsp. vanilla extract

1 Tbsp. raw honey (optional)

½ cup chopped dates, figs, or raisins

1. In a mixing bowl, combine all ingredients until well blended.
2. Divide among 12 greased or lined muffin cups.
3. Bake at 350°F for 20 minutes or until golden brown.

Hijiki Seaweed Oat & Nut Bars

2½ cups gluten-free oats

⅔ cup natural peanut butter (peanuts should be the only ingredient)

1 medium mashed banana

½ cup local honey

½ cup sunflower seeds (pumpkin seeds work well too)

1 cup raisins (chopped dates or figs work well too)

½ cup pastured melted local butter

½ cup Hijiki Seaweed

1 Tbsp. vanilla extract

1. In a large mixing bowl, combine all ingredients, mixing well.
2. Grease an 8 × 8 baking dish.
3. Spread granola mixture into dish and press down.
4. Bake on 350°F for 30 minutes. Cool completely and cut into squares.

Pumpkin Cake

1 box yellow organic cake mix

1 cup pumpkin purée

1 Tbsp. cinnamon

1. Mix cake mix with pumpkin purée and cinnamon until well blended (do not include ingredients on box).
2. Bake cake batter according to package directions.

Frozen Smoothie Pops

Why not jump on the smoothie bandwagon? The smoothies in this book are great breakfast treats. Kids like them because they are a frozen pop. Moms like them because they offer a unique but fun way to add more nutrients.

Mango & Pineapple Pop

2 cups frozen mango

2 cups frozen pineapple

½ tsp. grated ginger

1. Blend all ingredients until smooth and thick.
2. Pour into paper cups or frozen pop molds (makes 3 large or 6 small paper cups).
3. Freeze with wooden craft sticks for 4 hours.

Mango & Yogurt Pop

2 cup frozen mangos

1 plain or vanilla whole-fat yogurt

1. Blend all ingredients.
2. Pour into paper cups or frozen pop molds (makes 3 large or 6 small paper cups).
3. Freeze with wooden craft sticks for 4 hours.

Berry Greek Yogurt Pop

2 cups whole-fat vanilla Greek yogurt

2 cups frozen mixed berries

1. Blend all ingredients. Pour into paper cups or frozen pop molds (makes 3 large or 6 small paper cups).
2. Freeze with wooden craft sticks for 4 hours.

Kiwi & Banana Pop

2 bananas

4 kiwis (one for garnish)

1. Blend banana and kiwi together. Pour into paper cups or frozen pop molds (makes 3 large or 6 small paper cups).
2. Thinly slice one peeled kiwi. Slide kiwi slices down the sides of mold or cups.
3. Freeze with wooden craft sticks for 4 hours.

Green Machine Smoothie Pop

2 very ripe bananas

1 ripe avocado

1 cup kale leaves

½ cup applesauce

¼ cup water

1. Blend all ingredients. Pour into paper cups or frozen pop molds (makes 3 large or 6 small paper cups).
2. Freeze with wooden craft sticks for 4 hours.

Food Safety Warnings

It is essential that you wash all baby food preparation and serving equipment well with hot and soapy water.

WARNING: When using formula with well water, preparing your own baby food, or feeding before 3 months of age: Infant methemoglobinemia (nitrate poisoning) leads to cyanosis in infants with few clinical symptoms (blue baby syndrome). Nitrate Poisoning is the inability of the baby's red blood cells to be transported to the cells and tissues in the body. Sources of nitrites are in well water, and specific foods. If you are formula feeding, have your well water tested for nitrates routinely.

Top 10 Food Safety Tips:

- Wash your hands with hot, soapy water before preparing and serving food. Don't forget to wash your hands thoroughly between handling raw and cooked foods.
- Wash all equipment and surfaces with hot soapy water. If the equipment comes apart, disassemble before washing. Air dry on counter on a clean cotton towel.
- Wash and scrub all fruits and vegetables.
- Use high-quality ingredients that have been stored at the appropriate temperatures (between 35–38°F).
- Cook meat to a proper temperature of at least 165°F. Use a properly celebrated thermometer to gauge temperature.
- Steam, roast, bake, or broil to maintain maximum nutrients in food. If you boil fruit and vegetables, the nutrients leach into the water. If this is your preferred method, use the cooking water to thin large purée batches before freezing.
- Don't serve the same food twice with baby food. Discard leftover food in the baby's dish.
- Never leave baby food out at room temperature for more than 2 hours.
- Grind hard food (nuts, seeds) until smooth to prevent choking.
- Store food in the refrigerator for up to 48 hours. Store frozen purées in the freezer for up to 6 months.

Chapter 5 References

1. R. Sakashita, N. Nouse, and T. Kamegai, "From Milk to Solids: A Reference Standard for the Transitional Eating Process in Infant and Preschool Children in Japan," *European Journal of Clinical Nutrition*, 58 (2004): 643–53.

2. A. Ruzin and R.P. Novick, "Equivalence of Lauric Acid and Glycerol Monolaurate as Inhibitors of Signal Transduction in Staphylococcus Aureus." *Journal of Bacteriology*. 182 no. 9 (2000): 2668–71. http://www.ncbi.nlm.nih.gov/pubmed/10762277.

3. D.O. Ogbolu, A.A. Oni, O.A. Daini, A.P. Oloko, "In Vitro Antimicrobial Properties of Coconut Oil on Candida Species in Ibadan, Nigeria." *Journal of Medicinal Food*. 10 no. 2 (2007): 384–87. http://www.ncbi.nlm.nih.gov/pubmed/17651080.

4. Jon. J. Kabara, Dennis M. Swieczkowski, Anothony J. Conley, and Joseph P. Truant, "Fatty Acids and Derivatives as Antimicrobial Agents," *Antimicrobial Agents and Chemotherapy*. 2 no. 1 (1972): 23–28. http://www.ncbi.nlm.nih.gov/pmc/articles/PMC444260/.

Acknowledgments

This book has been years in coming, both in my dreams and from the encouragement of my family, friends, clients, and colleagues. Your support made this a reality.

To the entire Cedar Fort team—Hannah Ballard and Joanna Barker (Acquisitions Editors), Rozelle Hansen (Publicist), Bekah Claussen (Designer), and Rachel Munk (Editor) for supporting my idea and embracing this book with open arms. I appreciate your commitment, support and guidance through the entire process.

Margaret Loesch, I am thankful for your generosity and willingness to be a part of this book. Your feedback and advice has been extremely helpful. I am forever indebted to you.

My blog website designer, Shay Bocks (http://shaybocks.com), your work is unparalleled to any blog designer. And a huge thank you to all of the artists who contributed to the photography work in this book and my professional pictures: April Carpenter (http://www.aprilcarpenterphoto.com), Paul Steinruck (http://www.stoneridgeportraits.com), and Brianna Collins (www.briannacollins.me).

Thank you to all of my cute models: Hailey, Freya, Naomi, Samantha, Luca, Sofia, Genevieve, Louis, Ava, Margaret, Hannah Mae, Rose, Ignatius, Locklyn, Avery, Elizabeth, Adalyn, Kennedy, Dylan, and Cash.

To my children's teachers, you taught me to listen to my children and to understand them for who they are. You opened my eyes to their true capabilities and made me a better mother. Thank you to Margaret McCann and Rebecca Scavone (Wyoming Seminary), and Julie Pickarski and Nancy Fino (Wyoming Valley Montessori School).

To everyone who proofed the manuscript and allowed your children to be the taste testers: Dr. Jessica Bachman, Stacy Jenkins, Robyn Athearn, Elizabeth Derry, and Mindy Harrison.

I appreciate all of my colleagues and friends who are both near and far. I respect your willingness to talk through many controversial nutrition topics and show me the ropes. I know many of you endured countless conversations about book writing and infant feeding. You have all shaped this book in your own right: Dr. Joan Grossman, Dr. Joan Greulick, Dr. Diana Cuy Castellanos, Debra A. Pellegrino, Dr. Scott Breloff, Andy Stuka, Suzanne Kelly, Natalia Stasenko (www.tribecanutrition.com), Elizabeth Ward, Sally Kuzemchak (www.realmomnutrition.com), Sandy Watson, Rachel Russ, Jessica Badzio, April Rudat (http://www.dietitianapril.com), Jean Gruber, Megan Galko (www.nepamom.com), and Maryann Tomovich Jacobsen (www.raisehealthyeaters.com).

To my chosen sisters and lifelong friends, you not only encourage and support me in my everyday life, but you make me be a better person. Whether we are being adventurous in the kitchen, experiencing the same parenting trench war, or sharing a long swim, you keep the humor alive and my head above water: Katy Bradley, Jama Smith, Maria Myers, Betty Jo Adkins, Jill Turbyfill, Meghan Smith, Stacy Jenkins, Cathy Smith, Shannon Graham, Lori DeAngelo, Rachelle Rosencrance, Nicole Patrick, Patti Loyack, Diona Pavinski, Lisa Dennis, Kelly Dragwa, Keri McDermott, Melanie Matthews Damico, Kelly Ciravalo, Julie Pias, John McGurk, Ami Zachetti, Jolene Spadafora, Tammy Relick, and Alicia Kent.

To my aunts: Brenda Dolfi, Julie Turbyfill and Charlotte Farley, you all give me reasons to accept the challenges of life, in both the darkest and brightest of days. Your love, guidance, and spirituality are all a blessing in my life.

And to my amazing parents who saw the dream come alive day in and day out. Barbara and Ernie Gelb, thank you for always being there to watch your grandchildren on a moment's notice. You gave me a strong foundation of healthy eating habits. I not only love a variety of foods, but also have a healthy relationship with it because of you. You made family meals work even on the busiest days, and kept our southern roots alive. We ate kale before it was a fad, because you believed in linking us to your family traditions. Bill and Beth Cash, you gave me the courage to embrace cooking at a young age. I was listening on that hot day in Giddings, Texas, when you told me that good cooking is simply combining ingredients you like. You taught me to explore in the kitchen and provided me with the confidence many years ago to write this book today. Each of you provided me with support and encouragement to follow all of my dreams.

And to all four brothers, you continue to teach me that our relationships make us who we are today. Matt Cash, Michael Cash, Damon Gelb, and Ben Gelb, you are the best brothers a girl could ask for in life.

To my husband, David, for his endless ability to support and embrace all of my crazy ideas and projects. I am forever grateful to you and appreciate everything you do for our family. You are my life and love. You are the best father our children could ask for, and I love you with all of my heart.

To my children, Dylan and Cash, you have taught me the virtues of patience, understanding, and love. I experience the world through your eyes, and find a new laughter in everything we do because of you.

Index

RECIPE INDEX

KEYWORD INDEX

About the Author

Clancy Cash Harrison, MS, RD, LDN, a registered dietitian and pediatric feeding therapist, is on mission to help families raise healthy eaters. She provides parents with simple approaches to develop a positive relationship with food starting at birth. Clancy believes food should be fun and adventurous, not stressful and complicated. Working closely with families, she concentrates on "teaching taste" through food exploration and sensory experiences. Clancy currently lives in Pennsylvania with her husband and two children.